CIRCULAR WALKS
IN GWENT

Circular Walks
in Gwent

Richard Sale

GWASG Carreg
Gwalch

ISBN: 0-86381-479-4

Cover design: Alan Jones

First published in 1998 by Gwasg Carreg Gwalch,
12 Iard yr Orsaf, Llanrwst, Wales LL26 0EH
☎ (01492) 642031
Printed and published in Wales.

Contents

The Walks

LOCATION MAP

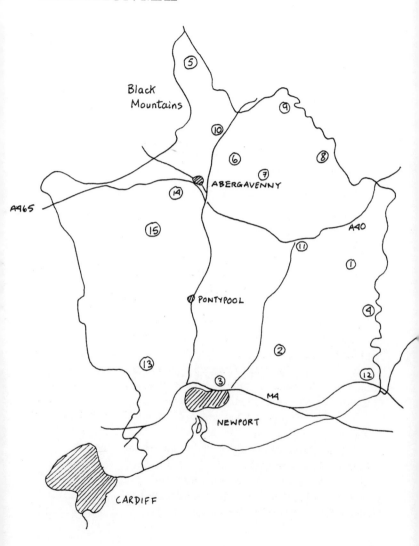

Introduction

The Guide

One of the aims of this guide is simplicity. Walks are easy to follow, and clear directions are given. Another aim is variety. Walks have been selected that will highlight Gwent's outstanding history and scenic beauty. The exact location for the starting point of each walk is given, and how to get there.

Walks vary in length from 2.5 miles/4 kilometres to 13 miles/21 kilometres. In general the walks are well maintained and clearly signposted. Many utilise waymarked long-distance footpaths, including sections of the Offa's Dyke National Trail. Those people uncertain of how long a walk of given length will take should use the Naismith Formula, a well-known walking aid. This suggest a time of one hour for every 3 map miles (or five map kilometres) covered, plus an additional half-hour for each 1,000 feet (300m) of ascent. The map distance is quoted for each of the walks, only one of which (Walk 5) involves significant climbing: Walk 5 includes 1,500 feet of ascent.

Sketch maps for each walk are provided - all, except Walk 4 (based on scale 1:50 000), are based on the 1:25 000 series; however they can be no substitute for the definitive OS (Ordnance Survey) maps. The walks are covered by Landranger sheets 161, 162, 171. At the larger scale the walker is helped by many of the walks being covered by Outdoor Leisure Sheets 13 and 14, though some of the walks require Pathfinder sheets. Please note that at the time of writing it is anticipated that these sheets will be replaced by sheets of the Explorer series (at the same scale) within a matter of months.

The grading system used is largely self-explantory. Easy walks involve short walks over easy terrain, with limited climbing. Moderate walks are either longer, have more climbing, or involve more complicated route finding. The strenuous routes are much longer or involve significant climbing.

For each walk the 'facilities' indicate whether food and drink are available on, or close to, the route. Those villages or towns noted as having full facilities are also likely to have public toilets and public transport, though the latter may be restricted to a few (or even just one) bus per day, and to offer accommodation. For a full list of accommodation options, contact the local Tourist Information Office.

Apart from Walk 5 none of the routes cross an upland area exposed to the weather - Walks 6 and 14 also cover upland areas, but are short and walkers are unlikely to be caught out by an unexpected storm. The remaining walks are low level and rarely remote. Nevertheless, all the walks will seem long and arduous to those ill-equipped for rain, cold or wind. Please ensure you are wearing or carrying adequate clothing and have proper footwear. And please remember to follow the Country Code.

Gwent: A Short History

In a book of history walks it seems inappropriate to also have a chapter dedicated to the history of Gwent. But Gwent is so important to the history of Wales that an overview of Welsh history is needed to place the historical snap-shots given in the walks in context. Gwent was - is - the borderland between Wales and England and saw the ebb tides of conquerors from the west, and the flow of Welshmen to the east. When it was formed Gwent incorporated the old county of Monmouthshire, a county whose folk sometimes seemed confused about their identity. And sometimes ambivalent too. There were road signs then that read 'Welcome to Monmouthshire and Wales'. Sometimes the 'and Wales' would be daubed out. Sometimes 'Wales' would be replaced by 'England'. And then others would undo the change. Gwent, it seems, has a better defined identity. But it is still a county which looks east to the *Cymry*, and yet takes the occasional long look over its shoulder just in case.

Gwent has probably been occupied by men for 250,000 years, though the occupation has not been continuous, the ice ages pushing polar ice southwards and forcing man to retreat over the land bridge that then joined south-east England to the continent. The earliest occupation has not resulted in recognisable remains: earliest man left few clues to his existence, and what he left may well have been rubbed away by the glaciers. The first remains so far discovered of man in Wales are from the Palaeolithic (Old Stone) Age, remains which are perhaps 20,000 years old. The best of these are the so-called Red Lady of Paviland, the skeletal remains (actually of a man, the bones stained with red ochre) found on the Gower, though other finds from the same era have been discovered at Arthur's Cave, in the Wye Valley near Symond's Yat. As Palaeolithic man was a hunter, it is likely that the tribe who occupied the Wye Cave also trod the soil of Gwent.

Palaeolithic remains are rare, in part because of the minimal use of tools which survive periods of 20,000 years or so, in part because although the folk were cave dwellers, they may not have always left the bodies of the dead close to the living. It is also likely that the settlement of the county was minimal: the ice ages were still grumbling on, with much of northern Britain being Arctic tundra and even the south a cold place, a difficult place to survive. Only on the coastal plain of Glamorgan does it seem that man could exist, and then, perhaps, only as a scattering of small communities.

But the climate was improving. The ice moved north and behind it forests started to colonise the tundra. More animals crossed the land bridge from Europe and with them came more advanced folk, a people who could start to leave their mark on the landscape. Neolithic (New Stone Age) folk buried their dead - the important ones at least - in chambers built of stone slabs which they earthed over to form long barrows. Sometimes time blew the earth away leaving behind a dolmen (or *cromlech* as it is known in Welsh). There are no good examples in Gwent, though close to Cardiff there are several - at Tinkinswood the long barrow is complete, while at St Lythans only the cromlech remains.

The Bronze Age brought a change of burial ritual, with cremation and the internment of ashes in cairns or round barrows. The Bronze Age was also the age of standing stones - though this might have been a continuation of earlier practice. The Welsh for a standing stone is *maen hir*, long stone, and it is that name, shortened to menhir, that has become popular in describing such stones. Lately, with the increased coverage - not all of it useful - given to astro-archaeology, menhirs have taken on a considerable significance. It is now possible to view the stones as markers of extraterrestrial air terminals, batteries holding mystical power, or connections for large energy reservoirs. While such

9

'earth magic' ideas may be too fanciful, it is easy to understand the emotional tug of such stones.

The replacement of the Bronze Age culture in Wales by the Iron Age people appears to have been by intermixing rather than annihilation. This theory rests on two bases: first the finding, in Llyn Fawr, Glamorgan, of a hoard of metal objects, some of bronze, some of iron and yet of, apparently, contemporary manufacture and usage; and secondly, and more romantically, the possibility of a real folk memory behind the story of the lady of the lake at Llyn y Fan Fach on Mynydd Du, to the east. The Iron Age in Wales is deeply significant as it represents the coming of the peoples whose name is synonymous with the country - the Celts.

To the civilised Romans and Greeks of Mediterranean Europe the Celts were barbarians, war-like savages. By comparison, of course, these descriptions were true, inter-tribal warfare being the apparent hallmark of the Celts (and later the downfall of the British), who also possessed no written language and worshipped strange gods. The Roman expansion into northern Europe was probably motivated as much by frequent attacks from the Celts on their border as by any expansionist dreams. The Romans were impressed by the qualities of the Celts in battle, but unimpressed by what they saw as the puerile boasting of their leaders, parading about in ornaments accompanied by men forever chanting their praises. They did not realise then the true significance of what they saw. The Celts, having only oral literature, had invested the history of their peoples in epic poems that were remembered and delivered by bards. This had two direct results. Firstly a heroic leader stock was created which continually broadcast their own, and their ancestors', heroism. Thus a leader who was not rich and majestic, and not celebrated in the bardic poems, was suspect and might not protect you well enough. Secondly a love of language for its own sake developed. To such an extent was this true that the Celts actually had a god of eloquence - Ogmios. Eventually the Romans and Greeks recognised this eloquence for what it was. The Celts maintained, in essence, that the tongue was mightier than the sword and they venerated age which increased its powers. Eventually they emerged in the classical world as teachers of rhetoric.

The Celtic tribes had invaded Britain at any early time and were well established when the Romans came: in many parts of Wales their typical hill fort can be seen. In 43AD the Romans subdued the Celts of southern England after many bloody battles, but one tribal leader, Caratacus, escaped to Wales where he rallied the Silures of south Wales and the Ordovices of the north. He fought on until 51AD when he was betrayed and captured. It seems that his fighting ability and his bearing after capture so impressed the Romans that he died peacefully as an honoured guest of Rome. During the battle for south Wales the Romans built Caerleon, one of the finest Roman sites in Britain. Gwent also boasts Caerwent, a site which is almost as impressive.

After subduing south Wales the Romans pressed on to Anglesey to destroy the seat of the Celtic priest class, the druids. Tacitus portray the sad scene of the soldiers of Rome confronted by the priesthood, whose only weapon was ritual cursing: the anger of Celtic deities proved no match for the short sword.

After the Roman conquest Britain was quiet for several centuries, the local Celtic tribes becoming Romanised and the basis of the present system of roads and towns being created. When the Romans finally withdrew, however, the Brythoniaid *(Britons)* proved that they had learnt nothing in the occupation years and there was an immediate return to tribalism with new kings emerging to do battle with each other. Such a system of small states with little cohesion and occasional open hostility was easy to deal with, and the Anglo-Saxon invaders pushed the British farther and farther west after the Romans departed. The Saxon advanced was halted for a while - possibly by the legendary King Arthur - but in 577 they won the battle of Dyrham, near Bristol, cutting the country in half and banishing the British to Cornwall and Wales. The Saxons saw the Brythoniaid to the west of the Severn as the *Wallas* - foreigners, a name deriving another Celtic tribe, the Velcae. The British, now isolated from their own kind, increasingly stopped referring to themselves as *Brythoniaid,* being instead 'fellow countrymen' - Cymry.

The foreigners of Wales were now left in peace while the Saxons moved northward to secure that border. This was a long process and the Saxons lost interest in westward expansion. Eventually an effective demarcation line was set up between Saxon England and Wales by the construction of a boundary dyke by the Mercian king Offa, though the true reason for its construction is not known.

Behind the dyke the Welsh were embracing Christianity, a succession of Celtic saints evangelising the country from the time of the Roman departure. Indeed, two of Britain's earliest Christian martyrs, Aaron and Julius, were executed at Caerleon in the 3rd century. But the Celts also continued to fight among themselves, no ruler of one of the great kingdoms - Gwynedd, Powys, Dyfed and Gwent, now the names of the Welsh counties - being able to unify the country. The northern kingdoms were occasionally brought under one man's control, but the southern counties, and particularly Gwent, maintained a stubborn independence. Eventually Gruffudd, son of Llywelyn ap Seisyllt did unify the country, in 1041, but he over-reached himself, seeking allegiances with Saxon lords near the dyke, probably in an effort to expand eastward. Earl Harold Godwinson convinced Edward the Confessor that the Welsh king represented a threat and received permission to move against him. Earl Harold invaded Wales killing Gruffudd. Wales fragmented again and by the time the Normans arrived at the dyke there was once more a system of small, usually squabbling kingdoms on its western side.

The Normans did not attempt a conquest of Wales, it apparently not being part of William's plan for his new realm. Instead the Conqueror installed a line of barons on the march, or boundary, of England and Wales. These lords ruled virtually independent states, and their westward boundaries were of their own choosing. Consequently they encroached on Welsh land perpetually, gradually pushing the "free" Welsh back. This strategy resulted in Gwent's Three Castles, built to protect the march lands from Welsh incursions.

Owain Gwynedd pushed the Normans back in Powys, but was defeated and forced back. Typically, Owain's death caused a power struggle and a weakening of Gwynedd, the most powerful of the Welsh kingdoms, but his grandson Llywelyn ap Iorwerth (Llywelyn the Great) succeeded to the kingdom in 1203 and strengthened it. He conquered Powys and by siding with the English barons gained rights for Wales in Magna Carta. He had successes in South Wales, including Gwent where he assisted the Marcher Lord Richard Marshall to recover Usk castle from Henry III. When Llywelyn died in 1240 Wales, while not unified, had a truly independent air, though the position of the south, and particularly of Gwent, was still ambiguous, the co-operation, however suspicious, between the Marcher lords and the Welsh leaders making full support for an independent Wales grudging at best.

In the wake of Llywelyn's death Wales fragmented again. His grandson, Llywelyn ap Gruffudd *(Llywelyn the Last),* campaigned again for Welsh unity: he demanded, and received, the title of Prince of Wales from Henry III under the treaty of Montgomery of 1267, but the king's son, Edward I, was made of sterner stuff than his predecessors. He invaded Wales, forcing a submission and homage from Llywelyn and imposing, with the Treaty of Aberconwy in 1277, a reduction of Llywelyn's postion to that of a baron. In 1282 Llywelyn rose again, but briefly, being killed in a minor skirmish near Builth Wells.

Edward built the castles of the 'Ring of Stone' to enforce English dominance. He also systematically removed the lineage of the Welsh royal houses by forcing women into nunneries and preventing men from producing heirs by long-term imprisonment or death. He also gave the Welsh a prince 'who could speak no word of English', a gesture which seems to have been appreciated at the time despite the modern view. Edward's imposed peace lasted 100 years before being shattered by the rebellion of Owain Glyndŵr. As with earlier Welsh princes, Glyndŵr's successes were mostly in the north, his forays into the south, particularly into Gwent being failures - as we shall see.

Glyndŵr's rebellion left Wales and the Welsh exhausted. But before the century was out the Welsh family of Tudor supplied England and Wales with a king when, in 1485, Harri Tudur became Henry VII. Thereafter Welsh history and English history coincide politically.

Socially that was not quite so, however, with rural Wales being a poor country until very recent times. The industrialisation of south Wales, the age of coal and steel, is usually seen as a Glamorgan valleys phenomenon, but Gwent played its part. Indeed, at Blaenafon, Gwent has the one of the most important - some would argue the most important - sites from that industrialisation.

The walks in this book explore all these periods in the history of Wales and Gwent, starting with the menhirs of Trelech and finishing, not surprisingly, at Blaenafon.

Country Code

Enjoy the countryside and respect it's life and work.
Guard against all risk of fire.
Fasten all gates.
Keep your dogs under close control.
Keep to the public paths across farmland.
Use gates and stiles to cross fences, hedges and walls.
Leave livestock, crops and machinery alone.
Take your litter home.
Help to keep all water clean.
Protect wildlife, plants and trees.
Take special care on country roads.
Make no unnecessary noise.

Welsh Place Names

Place names can be a fascinating study in their own right, indicating geographical features, patterns of former land ownership, forgotten buildings or former trades. However, the current place name may be far removed from the original name, particularly where there is an anglicised form of an old Welsh name e.g Pembroke is derived from Pen Fro, the Welsh for Land's End. Welsh place names are particularly expressive of geography, and can be highly poetic e.g. Pwll Deri, *pool of the oak trees*. Some of the more common names are listed below:

Aber — river mouth, estuary
Afon — river
Allt — wood, hill, slope
Bach/Fach — little
Bedd — grave
Bryn — hill
Bwlch — pass
Caer(au) — fort(s)
Canol — middle, centre
Capel — chapel
Carn — cairn
Carreg, pl. cerrig — rock, stone
Castell — castle
Cemais — river bend
Cleddau — sword
Coch — red
Coed — wood
Coetan — quoit
Cors — bog, marsh
Craig — rock, cliff
Crib — ridge
Croes — cross
Cromlech(au) — burial mound(s)
Cwm — valley
Cwrw — beer

Cyhoeddus — public
Dan — under
Dau — two
Deri — oak
Dinas — hill fort
Dôl — meadow
Du, Ddu — black
Dŵr — water
Dyffryn — valley
Efail — smithy
Eglwys — church
Ffordd — road
Ffos — ditch, dyke
Ffynnon — spring, well
Gain — fair, fine, elegant
Garn — cairn
Gelli — grove
Glan — river bank
Gors — bog, marsh
Gwastad — level, flat
Gwaun — moor, meadow
Gwyn — white
Gwynt — wind
Hafod — summer dwelling
Hen — old

Hendre — winter dwelling
Isaf — lower
Llan — church
Llannerch — clearing, glade
Llyn — lake
Llwybr — path/track
Llwyd — grey
Maen — rock/stone
Maes — field
Mawr/Fawr — great, big
Melin — mill
Melyn — yellow
Moel/Foel — bare topped hill
Morfa — marsh
Mynach — monk
Mynachlog — monastery
Mynydd — mountain
Nant — brook, stream
Newydd — new
Nos — night
Ogof — cave

Parc — field, park
Pen — head, top
Penrhyn — promontory, headland
Pentre — village
Plas — hall
Pont — bridge
Porth — harbour
Pwll — pool
Rhiw — hill
Rhos — moorland
Rhyd — ford
Sych — dry
Tafarn — inn
Traeth — beach
Tref — town, hamlet
Tŷ — house
Uchaf — upper
Y, Yr — the
Yn — in
Ynys — island
Ysgol — school

A few notes on pronunciation may help:

c — k (hard)
ch — as in lo*ch*
dd — th as in *th*at
f — v
ff — f
g — g (hard)
ll — pronounce l, keep tongue in position at roof of mouth, and hiss!
the — th as in *th*ink

There are 7 vowels, a,e,i,o,u,w and y. Pronunciation may be long or short.

w may be as in pool, or pull e.g. *cwm* (coom) — valley
y may be as in fun, or pin e.g. *y*, *yr* (u, ur) — the, *dyffryn* (dufrin) —
valley.

Many Welsh words change their pronunciation and spelling under
certain circumstances e.g. the initial consonant of many words may
soften: b to f, c to g, m to f, p to b etc. Common examples of
mutations are *bach* (little) to *fach*; *mawr* (big) to *fawr*, *porth*
(harbour) to *borth*. Such mutations can make tracing words
through a dictionary a little problematic for the unitiated!

Tourist Information Centres
(* - open throughout the year. The remainder are open Easter-
September. In general, when open, the offices are open daily, 10am-
5.30pm.)

Abergavenny, Swan Meadow, Monmouth Road * 01873 857588
Caerleon, 5 High Street 01633 422656
Chepstow, Castle Car Park, Bridge Street * 01291 623772
Magor, First Services and Lodge,
 Junction 23A of M4 * 01633 881122
Monmouth, Shire Hall, Agincourt Square 01600 713899
Newport, Newport Museum and Art Gallery,
 John Frost Square * 01633 842962

Weather Services
Weathercall 0891 333111, then code 113 for Gwent

There is, unfortunately, no specific number for a weather report for the
Brecon Beacons National Park.

More Walks

Offa's Dyke National Trail
This official long-distance footpaths starts (or ends) in Gwent, at Sedbury Cliffs near Chepstow, traversing the county to reach the most easterly ridge of the Black Mountains. Here the Trail exits Gwent on its way to Prestatyn. The Trail is highlighted on the Outdoor Leisure sheets and will be featured on the new Explorer maps.

Three Castles Walk
This fine walk - which is featured in three of the walks described here - links the three Norman castles of Grosmont, Skenfrith and White Castle. Though short at 18 miles (29 kilometres) the walk passes through some fine country in northern Gwent.

Usk Valley Walk
This walk was developed by Gwent County Council and lies wholly within the county, starting at Caerleon and following the river closely to Abergavenny, a distance of 25 miles (40 kilometres). The Trail is highlighted on Outdoor Leisure Sheet 13. It will be featured on the new Explorer maps, but is not highlighted on the present Pathfinder maps.

Wye Valley Walk
Originally there were two walks, the Upper and Lower Valley Walks, but these have now been linked to create a fine 110 mile (176 kilometre) route from Rhayader to Chepstow, staying close to the river.

Trelech

OS Maps:	Landranger Sheet 162 (Gloucester and Forest of Dean) Outdoor Leisure Sheet 14 (Wye Valley and Forest of Dean)
Start:	Trelech Church
Access:	Trelech lies on the B4293 which links Monmouth and Chepstow, about 6 miles south of Monmouth.
Parking:	There is limited parking within the village: please park considerately. The Lion Inn, opposite the church, has a large car park, but permission to use this must be sought before use.
Grade:	Easy - field paths, with limited climbing, and road walking. The road walking is on quiet roads or wide verges.

Points of Interest:

1. St Nicholas' Church is a lovely building with a spire that acts as a landmark on the latter part of the walk. Inside it has several fine features: the stone font may be Saxon, as may the grave slab. Nearby is a remarkable sundial sculpted in 1689. Its base has relief representations of the village's antiquities (the Well, Harold's Stones and Tump Terrett), all of which are passed on the walk.

In the churchyard there is an equally extraordinary cross. Standing on top of five stepped pavements, the cross itself looks far too small for the structure and it has been suggested that it once had a third section to its shaft, positioned between the existing pair. The pavements are made of massive blocks, originally laid above ground, but the first level now partially sunk, almost below ground level at one corner. Various attempts have been made to level the pavements, stone wedges having been inserted between the levels. The cross shaft

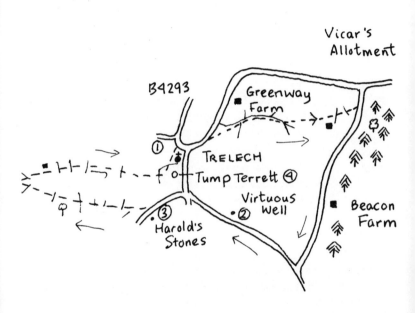

Vicar's Allotment

B4293

Greenway Farm

TRELECH

①

Tump Terrett ④

Virtuous Well
• ②

• ③
Harold's Stones

Beacon Farm

is hexagonal (an unusual feature as most shafts which were not circular were octagonal), the upper section tapered. It is topped by a small cross, itself an unusual feature as the majority of Gwent's (few) remaining crosses are topped by lanterns. The lantern heads were usually carved with Biblical figures, such crosses in churchyards being preaching crosses, the preacher taking the carved figures as the text of his sermon.

2. It is not clear when Trelech's holy or 'Virtuous' well was first enclosed. The Latin inscription on the sundial in the church notes it as one of the 'three wonders' of Trelech so it was certainly well known in the seventeenth century. The sundial also has two glasses, implying that the water was drunk. In 1708 Nathan Rogers noted that it was 'much frequented and found to be very Medicinal', while another writer noted that the water would 'expel ennui from the most desponding hypochondriac' so it was clearly by then seen as a spa water rather than a miraculous well. Yet the well structure has niches on either side. Such niches are usually associated with offerings, implying that at an earlier time the water may have had a reputation as miraculous. The water was certainly favoured by the local fairies, the village folk maintaining that on Midsummer's Eve the fairies danced around the well and, on Midsummer's Day, drank from it using harebells as cups.

3. Harold's Stones are a series of three standing stones aligned along a north-east/south-west path. The stones were such a feature of the landscape that they named the village - this is Tre Lech, the town of the stones. The present name of the village according to the Ordnance Survey (Trelleck) is merely an Anglicisation of the Welsh, avoiding the problems caused by the pronunciation of 'ch'. Harold's Stones are Neolithic or Bronze Age, meaning that they were erected 3,000 - 4,000 years ago. The stone are of the local rock, a conglomerate puddingstone, and so were not hauled any great distance, but there is evidence that the central stone has been chiselled to create its rounded shape. This stone also has two cup marks on its southern side. These marks, so called because of their resemblance to the bottoms of cups, are frequently seen on megaliths. It is assumed that the carvings

represent the sun. Although the stones are local, the effort involved in raising them should not be trivialised. The stones are all over 2m (6^1/$_2$ ft) high, and there is also a section buried below ground. They weigh several tons and bringing them to the site and erecting them required significant manpower and organisation. It is frustrating, therefore, to realise that almost nothing is known of the society that raised them. The alignment of the stones can hardly be accidental - there is no evidence that any of the stones have been moved - but neither the spacing nor the alignment has any obvious significance. In one sense, it is the very mystery of such stone placements that makes them so evocative and which leads them to 'alternative' belief systems. But the fact that so little is known about such sites does also make them very frustrating.

A local legend claims that the stones are the result of a game of quoits by Jack o'Kent, a local giant or wizard. Jack is said to have 'pecked' (thrown) the stones during the game. He is said to have actually thrown four stones, but one landed closer to Trelech village and fell over. It has now been moved (to help with the ploughing), but when it was in position it was known as the Pecked Stone.

The name of the stones is as mysterious as their origin. Often such sites are named for a mythical figure - Arthur is very popular - or to the Devil, but Harold is a very specific name. It is claimed that Harold Godwinson, the Harold who was killed at Hastings, won a battle here in the late Saxon period and that the stones took his name as a memorial. It is further claimed that Tump Terrett is the burial mound of the soldiers who died, and that a local field is known as Bloody Field because it was so soaked with blood that nothing but gorse will grow in it.

4. Tump Terrett is the remains of a 'motte and bailey' castle. These early Norman castles consisted of a flat-topped, steep-sided mound of earth - the 'motte' - on which a wooden tower or stockade was built. The mound was surrounded by a ditch which might be filled with water or sharpened sticks. The 'bailey' was a courtyard at the base of the mound defended by a rampart and ditch or a wooden fence. These early castles were later reinforced, the motte being topped, or replaced, by a stone tower (or keep), the bailey also being given a stone wall. The

best illustration of a motte and bailey becoming a stone-built castle is at Cardiff. At Trelech all that survives is the remnant motte, its surrounding ditch now only existing on its northern side. Nothing remains of the bailey.

It is not clear when the castle was constructed, but it is likely to have been in the late 12th or early 13th centuries when the area was controlled by the de Clare family whose main castle was at Usk. Trelech was then a flourishing town. By the end of the 13th century it was one of the largest in Gwent and by the 14th century it was one of the ten largest towns in Wales. It then declined sharply in prosperity.

Walk Directions   [-] denotes Point of Interest

1. Opposite the church [1] is the Lion Inn. Facing the inn, turn left, then right, leaving the main road through the village for a minor road heading east towards the Forest of Dean. After 150m, go right, climbing steps to reach a stile. Walk to the top left corner of the field beyond and go through the gate. Now follow the left edge of the next field to reach a stile on the left.

2. Cross and go half-right to reach a stile. Cross and bear left along a faint path to reach a stile over a wire fence. Cross and head uphill, aiming for the left edge of a barn to reach a stile. Cross and bear half left across a paddock to a stile across a wooden fence. Continue, crossing another stile then heading for a handy marker post. Maintain direction to reach a stile on to a road.

3. Turn right and follow the road, with an excellent piece of forest on the left and fine views over Trelech on the right. Go past Beacon Farm, left, and follow the road downhill to a T-junction. Turn right and follow the road towards the village. After 800m you will reach the Virtuous Well [2] on the right.

4. Continue along the road to reach a T-junction. Turn right, soon reaching a T-junction with the B4293. Turn left and follow the verge of the main road, soon reaching a kissing gate, on the left giving, access to Harold's Stones [3]. Continue along the main road for another 50m, then take the wide track on the right.

5. Follow the track for 250m to reach a signed track for Cwmcarfan Hill, on the right. Take this but after a few paces (just beyond the building on the left) go left, up steps and over a signed stile. Now follow the right field edge, using a stile and then a gate between fields. Go between a small copse (left) and the fence (right), pass a ruined barn and go down and right to reach a stile and footbridge. Continue with the fence on your right for 50m to reach a stile across it.

6. Cross and turn sharp right to reach a footbridge and stile. Follow the hedge (then fence) on the right to reach a ruined barn. Go through the gate to the right of this and follow the fence on the left to another gate. Maintain direction across the next field to reach a stile. Trelech Church spire is now visible. Head to the right of it, towards the farm, then towards Tump Terrett when it comes into view. Cross a stile beside a gate, then a stile across a hedge. Step right and cross a concrete bridge, then bear left, as signed, through the hedge line. Cross a stile into a paddock and go half-right to a stile in the far corner. Tump Terrett [3] is to the right here.

7. Turn left, crossing a ladder stile and stile and continuing (barn to the right) to another stile. Soon after this a step up right reaches the churchyard, though the path continues to the village road.

Facilities

There is an inn at Trelech.

Gray Hill

OS Maps:	Landranger Sheet 171 (Cardiff, Newport and surrounding area)
	Outdoor Leisure Sheet 14 (Wye Valley and Forest of Dean)
Start:	Foresters' Oaks
Access:	Take the minor road to Llanfair Discoed which leaves the A48 just west of Caerwent. Follow the road through the village and beside Wentwood Reservoir. Foresters' Oak is just beyond the reservoir, to the left.
Parking:	There is a car park at Foresters' Oaks.
Grade:	Easy - tracks and good paths, but a steep climb to the hill top. In wet weather the path to the summit can be very muddy: wait for a dry day, preferably a clear one to take advantage of the view.

Points of Interest:

1. Neolithic man buried his dead, but in the Bronze Age the corpse was cremated rather than interred. The ashes were then placed in a cyst, either a stone 'box' or a pottery vessel. In many upland sites the burial was marked by a cairn, a simple circular heap of stones familiar to all mountain walkers. Occasionally there was a more elaborate stone cyst, a 'box' of stones below the surface ringed by a bank or ditch. If the ring was of stones then the burial site is known as a ring cairn.

   The site on Gray Hill may be a ring cairn as there are two large stones at the ring centre which may have formed a burial cyst. Alternatively the 13 stones that now remain may have been a stone circle. None of these stones is large, the tallest being only ¹/₂ metre. But the Gray Hill site is not a simple circle or ring cairn. In addition to the two stones at the centre there is a tall (1.8m) standing stone to

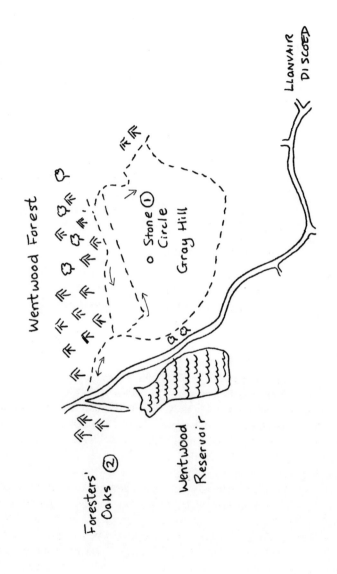

Wentwood Forest

Stone Circle ①
Gray Hill

Foresters' Oaks ②

Wentwood Reservoir

LLANVAIR DISCOED

26

the east of the circle, another to the south-east and a series of three stones forming an alignment to the north. Further north again is a tall (2m) standing stone. This is a very complex arrangement and clearly had enormous significance to those who built it. In the wake of the discovery of astronomical alignments at Stonehenge, other megalithic sites have been subjected to similar investigations, whether by professional or amateur astronomers. Here at Gray Hill it has been found that the two tall standing stones are aligned to the mid-winter sunrise. This seems to make the most sense for a superstitious, agrarian society. What would have concerned Bronze Age folk most as winter arrived and the days of sunlight shortened was that the days would eventually lengthen again so that crops could be sown. If, as is likely, the folk worshipped the sun, then the marking of mid-winter, probably with rituals and sacrifices of some form, would have been of paramount importance. It is sad that these ideas about the alignment cannot be confirmed and that the details of the rituals carried out at such sites will never be known.

From the top of the hill the view southward is marvellous, taking in the southern Gwent plain and the Bristol Channel. On clear days Somerset's Mendips and Quantock Hills are visible.

2. The information boards at the car park include a section on old expressions used by forest dwellers when Wentwood Forest stretched from the Usk to the Wye. Most intriguing is that in medieval times a special court was held to try those who had broken forest laws on animal grazing, wood collecting etc. The court was held twice each year at a group of trees known as Foresters' Oaks. It is thought that these oaks stood at the car park which now bears the name.

Walk Directions   [-] denotes Point of Interest

1. From the car park go back to the road and bear right across it to reach a signed track. Follow this for 500m to reach a track junction. To the left is the return route: continue ahead for 250m to reach a rising path on the left. Take this, following it steeply uphill. There is a path fork near the top, with a trench-like path going off to the left: this can be taken, but it is best to stay with the main path.

2. The path crosses the top of the hill, but keeps to its northern edge. To reach the stone circle it is necessary to bear right through the bracken. There are numerous paths here, some cut by mountain bikes/ scramblers. Not all of these are helpful, but they make directions useless. The stone circle and standing stones lie just over the southern edge of the long summit ridge, about 300m from where the path reaches the summit plateau (and about 200m to the south of it).

3. Continue along the clear summit path, descending the hill's eastern edge to reach a crossing track. It is possible to turn left or right here. The left turn offers the shortest way back to the start - though many walkers will just reverse the outward route from the stone circle. Turn left and follow the wide track around the northern base of Gray Hill, rejoining the outward route at the track junction. Turn right to return to Foresters' Oaks [2].

Facilities

There is a picnic site at Foresters' Oaks. There is an inn at Llanfair-Discoed on the road from the A48 to the start.

Caerleon

OS Maps:	Landranger Sheet 171 (Cardiff, Newport and surrounding area)
	Pathfinder Sheets 1130 (Cwmbrân) and 1149 (Newport)
Start:	The Roman Amphitheatre, Caerleon
Access:	Caerleon lies on the B4236 just a short distance north of Newport, from which it is well signposted. The town is close to Junction 24 of the M4 and to the A449 dual carriageway which links Raglan, Monmouth and Ross-on-Wye with Newport.
Parking:	There is parking at the Roman Amphitheatre.
Grade:	Easy - field paths and roads. But there is some climbing, and the final exit on to the road needs great care.

Points of Interest:

1. The Arthurian legends are part of the Welsh cultural heritage, the country being dotted with sites named for the heroic king. Dinas Emrys in the Snowdonia National Park is associated with Merlin, and Arthur himself is said to sleep in a cave hidden in Lliwedd's cliffs awaiting the call to return and save Wales. Most people are familiar with Camelot, the Round Table and the exploits of the chivalrous knights, but not everyone is aware that these are medieval versions of older folk tales, thickly overlaid with later romantic notions. The original tales, as organised by Geoffrey of Monmouth and then taken up by the French poet Chrétien de Troyes (who altered them and re-exported them to Britain), have a less romantic, but far more mystical, tone. And these early stories place the Court of Arthur at *Caer Llion* - Caerleon. Geoffrey's version of the Arthurian stories has Arthur crowned here and his knights leaving for their adventures from Caerleon. Only with Mallory's reworking of the stories, in *Le Morte d'*

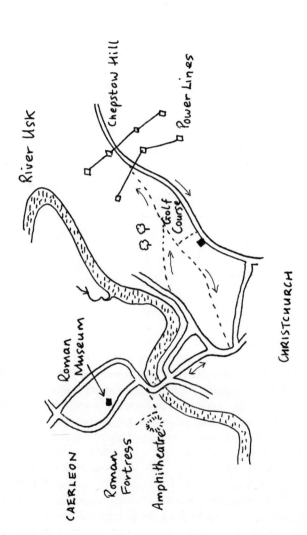

River Usk

Chepstow Hill

Power Lines

Golf Course

CHRISTCHURCH

Roman Museum

CAERLEON

Roman Fortress

Amphitheatre

30

Arthur, does the idea of Camelot take hold: Mallory places Camelot at Winchester, moving it from a far-flung ancient fortress to the old capital of royal England. This romanticism was pushed to the limit by Tennyson in his *Idylls of the King*, in which the Knights of the Round Table became the epitome of chivalry. Tennyson stayed at the Hanbury Arms in Caerleon while he was working on his poem.

Geoffrey's choice of Caerleon was no accident. Geoffrey's ancestors were Welsh - the Britons of Arthur's time - and he saw Arthur as the link between the civilisations of Rome and the Britons: each had succumbed to barbarians, the Britons to the Saxons and then to the Normans. Placing Arthur at Caerleon gave him continuity, for Caerleon had been a Roman fortress.

Caerleon is the Welsh version of the Latin *Castra Legiones*. This was the 'camp of the legions', the headquarters from 75AD onwards of the Second Augustan Legion and one of only three permanent legionary fortresses in Britain (the other two being at Chester and York). Within its 50 acres, about 6,000 of Rome's finest legionnaires were housed. The fort conformed to the standard Roman pattern. It was more or less square and surrounded by a deep, V-shaped ditch on the inside of which was an earth rampart topped by a wooden fence. At frequent intervals along the wall there were wooden watch-towers. Inside there were barracks in a strict grid pattern, houses for the commanders, a bath-house and a hospital. Although the original buildings were wooden, the fort was rebuilt in stone from about 100AD. The fort was extremely important when it was first built as the local Silure Celts were resisting the Romans, but by the 3rd century AD the area was relatively peaceful. At the end of that century the legion was moved and the fort was abandoned. After the Romans had gone the fort was probably used by the local Welsh, but as they were a less organised society it is likely that they saw it as a convenient quarry rather than a potential town site. By the 19th century the site had been covered by blown earth and the expansion of the medieval town of Caerleon. Periodically Roman finds were unearthed by farmers or householders, one classic story telling of a visiting historian finding an inscribed altar which had been cut into paving slabs.

In the 1920s Caerleon was excavated by the famous archaeologist Sir Mortimer Wheeler. It is now the finest Roman site in Britain, and one of the best understood. The best features are the amphitheatre and the bath-house: the amphitheatre was almost certainly part of the first phase of building, the Romans being keen to maintain the morale of troops in one of the Empire's furthest flung corners. It is the best preserved amphitheatre in Britain and a remarkable structure. When complete it would have had tiered wooden seats on top of the earth banks and a sand covered arena. The seats would have run above the entranceways to the arena and through those entrances would have come gladiators and wild animals, though the amphitheatre would also have been used for less flamboyant shows - military parades, religious services and weapons training. The amphitheatre was large enough to seat the entire legion. The bath-house has all the usual Roman Features - *nymphaeum* (fountain house), heated changing rooms, large bath, cold plunge bath and so on. The site museum includes a number of personal articles lost in the baths and collected in its drain.

The best of the finds from excavations at the Roman sites can be seen in the museum which stands opposite the turning to the baths and amphitheatre site.

2. The Usk Valley Walk links the Ship Inn Caerleon with the Usk Bridge at Abergavenny, a distance of 40 kilometres (25 miles). It is a fine walk offering great views of the valley and, in its later stages, tempting views of the Black Mountains.

Walk Directions   [-] denotes Point of Interest

1. Cross the stone, and then wooden, stiles and follow the signed path along the north-eastern (town's side) edge of the amphitheatre [1]. Beyond the site, either follow the left field edge, or step up left to walk along a section of the old wall. If in the field, soon turn left into another field. If on the wall, bear left with it, then descend rough 'steps' at the wall end into a field. Either route now crosses the field to reach a stile on to a road. Cross, with care, and turn right to reach the pedestrian walkway across Caerleon bridge.

2. Bear left to reach, and pass, the Ship Inn, then turn left along Lulworth Road, which is signed as part of the Usk Valley Walk [2]. Follow the road, bearing right into Isca Road (another memorial to the Romans, who also called Caerleon *Isca Silurum*). To the left there are fine views of the Usk. Follow the road to reach a T-junction opposite the Bell Inn which, as the notice states, lies on the site of a Roman cemetery. Turn left for 300m to reach a stile on the right (signed for the Usk Valley Walk). Cross this into a rather scruffy area - the next part of the walk follows the line of a Roman road to/from the Caerleon fort: the Romans would have been much tidier - and bear left to follow a faint, but distinct path through scrub, crossing two further stiles to reach a plantation of new trees. There are fine views of Caerleon to the left.

3. The path now climbs through the trees (some of which are oak, the druids' tree - planted to annoy Roman ghosts?) to reach a stile on to a new golf course. Turn left and follow the black- (then blue-) topped posts which mark the Usk Valley Walk around the course edge. Work in progress sometimes impinges on the Walk, but it is always easy to follow. Finally a new lake, to the right, is passed to reach another scruffy area: bear left to reach a stile on to a road, or cross this area directly on to the road.

4. Turn right, passing the new Celtic Manor Golf and Country Club, on the left, and, soon, the golf course, on the right. Just before a house on the right, cross the signed stile, also on the right, on to the course. The right of way bears left here, but the course owners have erected yellow posts to guide walkers to the stile passed on the outward journey. Follow these (first across grass, then down a metalled path), but before reaching the stile, bear left to reach a line of blue-topped yellow posts heading off to the left.

5. Follow the posts, with a hedge on your right, into a corner, and go left, up steps to reach a stile on the right. Cross and follow the clear path beyond downhill through good woodland. The path is stepped where steep and stepped again where it reaches the road. Please be cautious here as the bends to both left and right are blind. Cross the road, bearing right to reach a pavement. Follow the pavement back to

the Ship Inn, recross the bridge and reverse the outward route back to the amphitheatre.

Facilities

There is a full range of facilities at Caerleon, as well as the excellent Bell Inn along the walk.

Tintern Abbey

OS Maps: Landranger Sheet 162 (Gloucester and the Forest of Dean)
Outdoor Leisure Sheet 14 (Wye Valley and Forest of Dean)

Start: Tintern Abbey

Access: The abbey lies beside the A466, Chepstow to Monmouth road, a beautiful road which follows the Wye. Tintern Abbey is 6 miles/9¹/₂ kilometres from Chepstow.

Parking: There is a car park at Tintern Abbey.

Grade: Moderate - walking on easy paths, but with a steep ascent from, and a steep descent, to the river.

Points of Interest:

1. The abbey was founded in the 12th century, for Cistercian monks, by Walter de Clare, Lord of Chepstow, as a penance, probably for a killing (perhaps even of his wife). A local priest sent him on a crusade where he made repeated attempts to get himself killed, but returned unscathed to endow the abbey as a final penance. The abbey was rebuilt in the 13th century by Roger Bigod, Earl of Norfolk. The Earl obtained his curious surname from confrontations with his King. The King on one occasion shouted that Roger must go, or stay and be hanged. Roger replied, 'By God, Sir, I will neither go nor be hanged' and was Roger Bigod thereafter. There is, perhaps, evidence in the charter of grants to the abbey that Roger drew up, that he too was doing penance:

'Be it known to your community (of the church of St Mary de Tynterne)
that I, in the sight of God, and for the health of my soul, and the souls of my

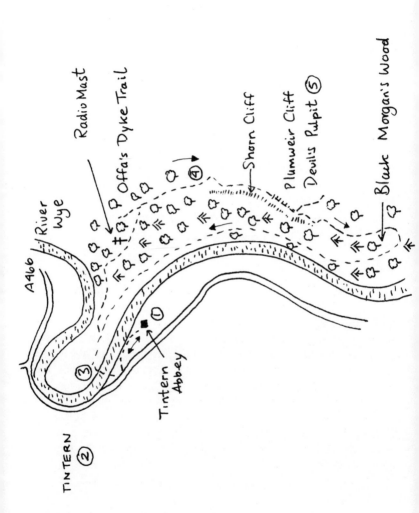

A466

River Wye

Radio Mast

Offa's Dyke Trail

Sharn Cliff

Plumweir Cliff

Devil's Pulpit ⑤

Black Morgan's Wood

④

Tintern Abbey

①

③

TINTERN ②

ancestors, and heirs, have confirmed to you divers lands, and possessions....'

After its dissolution, Tintern, like monasteries elsewhere, was stripped bare of its treasures and its roofing and then plundered for its stone.

It was as a ruin that Tintern attracted visitors in the late 18th century. At that time the well-off of Britain went on tours in search of the 'Picturesque'. Sites throughout Britain were scored on a points system which took into consideration the view, its framing, the colours and so on, all laid down in various publications, the most famous of which was that by the Rev. William Gilpin. Gilpin was especially fond of the Wye and recommended the Wye Tour, one of the highlights of which was Tintern Abbey. He noted: 'it has been an elegant Gothick pile', but added: 'though the parts are beautiful, the whole is ill-shaped. No ruins of tower are left, which might give form, and contrast to the walls, and buttresses, and other inferior parts. Instead of this, a number of gable ends hurt the eye with their regularity; and disgust it by the vulgarity of their shape. A mallet judiciously used (but who durst use it?) might be of service in fracturing some of them; particularly those of the cross aisles, which are not only disagreeable in themselves, but confound the perspective'.

The ruin which Gilpin and his fellow Tourers saw was ivy-clad. Now bare, it is possibly less romantic - though thankfully Gilpin never saw his wish of a judicious mallet realised - but still exquisite. The remains are sufficiently intact for a real appreciation of the monastery, its size and lay-out. The whole has been called the most beautiful ruin in Britain. When seen in the misty morning of a clear day with the leaves of the trees behind a summer green, or autumn gold, it is hard to disagree.

2. The name Tintern is from the Welsh *Din Teyrn*, a short form of Dinas Teyrn, the fortress of Teyrn, a king of Morgannwg (Glamorgan) who lived in about 600AD. The fortress of the name has not been discovered, but legend has it that it was besieged by the Saxons, and during the siege Teyrn was killed.

3. The monks are credited with bringing iron making to Tintern, though the site was an obvious one, there being not only local

ironstone, but vast forests for the production of charcoal. Only with the discovery of coal did the area decline in importance. Brass was first made in Britain at the Tintern metal works. Later the site was an important wire works, the old bridge over the Wye carrying a tramway into the site.

4. This section of Offa's Dyke is one of the finest which remain. The dyke was dug in the final years of the 8th century by the Saxon King Offa, though exactly why is still a cause for debate. The most likely suggestion is that it was a defensive barrier between the Saxons and the Welsh, its construction a unilateral decision by the Saxons seeking to put an end to Welsh incursions into the western part of their kingdom. It is an attractive idea, but up until then the Saxons had successfully pushed their border westwards - were they really that afraid of the remaining Celts in Wales, the tribes they had beaten so often? And did they, in any case, have the men to police such a defensive structure? - it is 160 miles/256 kilometres from Chepstow to Prestatyn. Other experts see the dyke as a negotiated frontier between the Welsh and the Saxons acting as a national boundary between the two, perhaps even as a trading line. In 796 the Saxon builders of the dyke had reached the Clwydian Mountains, just a few miles from Prestatyn and the sea. At that time Offa was killed near Rhuddlan in a skirmish with a Welsh army. It is said that the battle followed the breakdown of negotiations over the line the last section of dyke would take. If true, that seems to be carrying the definition of negotiation rather too far. Work stopped with Offa's death, the dyke never being completed.

5. The Devil's Pulpit, an isolated limestone pillar, is so named because it is said that the devil stood here and attempted to persuade the monks building the abbey to stop their work. As we have seen, the devil's 'preaching' did not work. The pulpit offers a wonderful view of the abbey (which is presumably why the devil chose it) and also of the Wye's wooded valley.

Walk Directions   [-] denotes Point of Interest

1. From the car park beside the abbey [1], walk towards the River

Wye, bearing left to walk with the river on you right. The path soon reaches the main road (the A466). Go right, with care, for 150 metres. The village of Tintern [2] is just ahead, but the route turns right along a wide path and goes over the old wire-works bridge [3].

2. Bear right along a track, following it for 400 metres to reach a stony track, on the left, reached between tall posts. Take this track, following it to reach a track fork near a bridge parapet.

3. Fork right and, after 50 metres, fork right again. Now, soon, turn left along a rocky track that climbs steeply and then becomes surfaced. The surfaced track also forks: take the left branch and climb steps to reach a wide, level forest track close to a radio mast.

4. Turn right, then almost immediately left and climb steadily through the wood to reach a tall signpost standing beside a very good section of Offa's Dyke [4]. Turn right, following both the dyke and the Offa's Dyke National Trail. About 70 metres beyond the next signpost, where you turn right, look right to see the Devil's Pulpit [5].

5. Continue along the dyke/National Trail, passing a memorial seat to Chris Pugh, a countryside warden, set where there is another wonderful view of the valley. About 800 metres from the Devil's Pulpit there is a sharp left turn: leave the dyke/Trail here, going straight ahead, descending through woodland.

6. Go down steps and continue to reach a forest track. Turn left and, after 100 metres, take a path on the right to continue descending. On reaching a wide forest track, go straight over, continuing to descend along a track which turns sharp right and, eventually reaches the trackbed of the old Wye Valley Railway, which was closed in 1964.

7. Turn right and follow the old railway trackbed. The railway curved right just before the abbey, crossing the river and continuing up its western side. However, a branch line continued to the old wire-works, and that is the return route: follow the trackbed, with the abbey and river close on your left, to regain the outward route near the old bridge.

8. Now reverse the outward route back to the start.

Facilities

There is a full range of facilities at the Abbey and in the village.

Llanthony

OS Maps:	Landranger Sheet 161 (Abergavenny and the Black Mountains)
	Outdoor Leisure Sheet 13 (Brecon Beacons National Park- Eastern Area)
Start:	Llanthony Priory
Access:	Llanthony Priory lies in the Vale of Ewyas on the eastern side of the Black Mountains. A road runs through the vale, climbing to Gospel Pass and then descending to Hay-on-Wye. The southern end of the Vale is reached by a minor road that leaves the A465 (Abergavenny-Hereford road) at Llanfihangel Crucorney.
Parking:	There is a car park beside Llanthony Priory.
Grade:	Strenuous - begins on field paths, but then climbs steeply to, and follows, an exposed Black Mountains ridge. The descent is also steep, but the walk ends easily on field paths.

Points of Interest:

1. St David's Church, which serves the scattered community in the upper part of the Vale of Ewyas is named for Wales' patron saint because a local legend maintains that St David (Dewi Sant) spent time in the valley early in his life, living as a hermit. It is claimed that the valley's first church was built on the site of St David's hermit cell. This site, and the first church erected there, was a *llan*, the Welsh word describing a small religious centre covering everything from a single hermit's cell, through a community of monks to a church used by local families. St David's *llan* was beside the stream that runs through the valley, the Nant Honddu. So this was Llanddewi Nant Honddu, a name that was eventually shortened to Llanthony. In the 12th century the present church replaced the first one, but still stands

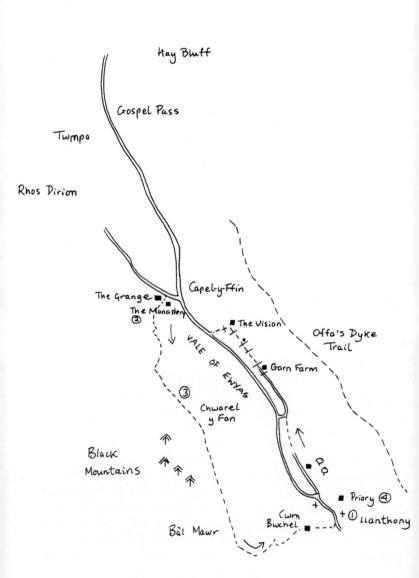

Hay Bluff

Gospel Pass

Twmpa

Rhos Dirion

The Grange

The Monastery ②

Capel-y-Ffin

VALE OF EWYAS

The Vision

Offa's Dyke Trail

Garn Farm

③

Chwarel y Fan

Black Mountains

Priory ④

Llanthony ①

Cwm Bwchel

Bâl Mawr

42

on the site of St David's cell. When the Priory was built the locals were allowed to worship in the Priory Church, and St David's Church became an infirmary, for both monks and locals. At the Dissolution, the Priory Church was sold as part of the monastery and the church became the parish church again.

2. The house to the left is Llanthony Monastery, a confusing name given that Llanthony Priory was itself a monastery. The name derives from the ownership of Joseph Leycester Lyne who was born in Barking in 1837. Lyne was ordained as a deacon in the Church of England in 1860, but felt so strongly that there was a need to re-establish Anglican monasticism in Britain that he moved to the Vale of Ewyas in 1870 and founded a House of Contemplation. Lyne built the Monastery, calling it Llanthony Tertia as it was the third monastic house to take the Llanthony name. Lyne changed his name to Father Ignatius and spent considerable time travelling and preaching, even going as far as the USA. Lyne used all the money he collected in the building of The Monastery, but the church he planned to stand beside the house remained unfinished when he died in 1908. Father Ignatius had received no support from the Anglican church, though he was ordained in his uncompleted church in 1898.

3. The Black Mountains are the third, and most easterly, great mountain block of the Brecon Beacons National Park (the others being the Beacons themselves and Mynydd Ddu, the western block). The park was designated in 1957 and covers over 1,300 square kilometres. Its uplands are composed of Old Red Sandstone from which a limestone cap has now all but eroded. In the Black Mountains, the limestone exists only on Pen Cerrig Calch on the range's westernmost ridge. This cap shines white in the sun, leading many who view the hills from near Crickhowell to think that there is a sprinkling of snow.

The Black Mountains form a series of long, broad ridges, like fingers, running north-south, parallel to each other. The joining knuckles of these fingers runs east-west at the range's northern end, this high east-west linking ridge being breached by Gospel Pass. The most exacting walk from Llanthony Priory is to climb eastwards on to the range's most easterly ridge and to follow it northwards. This walk follows the Offa's Dyke National Trail, with the left foot in Gwent and the right in Herefordshire initially, but soon with the left foot in Powys. At Hay Bluff, descend westwards to Gospel Pass and continue westwards to Point 713 near Rhos Dirion. Now follow the broad ridge southwards joining the present route near the Powys/Gwent border. This is a magnificent route, but at 20 miles (32kms) it is very exacting.

4. Legend has it that when William de Lacy, a retainer of the Earl of Hereford, was out hunting one day (in about 1100) he came across the Llanthony church. He was so entranced by the site, and by the Vale of Ewyas itself, that he repented his comfortable life as the servant of a lord and decided to become a hermit. The story says that William 'Instead of fine linen (he) covered himself with sackcloth, and instead of his soldier's robe he loaded himself with weighty irons'. Apparently, to increase his physical tortures William also wore his armour over his sackcloth, wearing it until it fell apart from rust.

De Lacy's lifestyle attracted attention and William Rufus' Queen sent her chaplain to visit him. The chaplain was equally entranced by the spot, and so caught up with William's religious fervour that he stayed. The Earl of Hereford then gave land and money to the hermits so that a monastery could be founded. In 1108 a new church was built and by 1120 the monastic buildings were complete. Llanthony Priory must have been a beautiful place: Gerald of Wales claims that when the Bishop of Salisbury, one of Henry I's chief ministers, visited the Priory he claimed that the King's treasury could not build a nave as grand as that offered by the hills that surrounded it. Unfortunately the beauty of the site and the magnificence of the priory were not sufficient to promote brotherly love. In 1136 there was a dispute that resulted in the monks being besieged by the locals. The origins of the dispute are not clear: some say it arose between the local Welsh and their Norman overlords - easy to understand as the latter treated the former little better than farm animals - while others claim it arose between local Welsh clans. Whatever the cause, the monks feared for their safety and, when the siege was lifted, they fled to Gloucester. To continue with their prayers and study the monks built a new Priory on the banks of the Severn, calling it Llanthony Secunda to make it clear that their

44

first home was in Ewyas. The monks certainly returned to Ewyas, a presence of some sort being maintained there. In 1175 new funds were granted for the rebuilding and refurbishment of the Priory, but perhaps by then, and certainly in the centuries that followed, Ewyas was an unpopular posting for the monks at Gloucester. And it was a compulsory posting for, as one young monk put it, 'who would choose to go and sing to the wolves'.

Gerald of Wales, writing perhaps 30 or 40 years after the monks had moved from Ewyas, was appalled. Gerald was part-Welsh, part-Norman, born in Manorbier Castle (in southern Pembroke) and with a hankering to be the Bishop of St David's Cathedral. It is thought likely that he spent some time in Llanthony during his youth: he certainly had a soft spot for the site - though who could blame him. Gerald wrote two books on Wales in the late 12th century, one a description of the country, the other a travelogue of his journey through Wales drumming up support for a Crusade. The treatment of the original Priory by the monks at Gloucester touched him deeply. The Ewyas Priory was, he said, 'formerly a happy, a delightful spot, most suited to the life of contemplation.' But it had now 'been reduced to servitude through the boundless extravagance of the English'. Gerald complained of 'uncontrolled ambition, the ever-growing vice of ingratitude, the negligence of its prelates and its patrons and, far worse than all of these, the fact that the daughter-house, become a step-mother, has odiously and enviously supplanted its own mother.' To add weight to this spleen-venting, Gerald noted the demise of some of the 'negligent prelates' of the Secunda. Prior William was expelled as unworthy, Prior Clement died after a paralysing stroke and Prior Roger died a miserable, lingering death. Gerald clearly saw poetic justice, if not actually God's hand in these events.

Of course, in the long term, it all mattered little, both Priories being dissolved by act of Henry VIII. At the time of its dissolution Llanthony had just five monks living there (and there had hardly been more in the preceding centuries) and was technically bankrupt. As elsewhere the dissolved Priory became a quarry for the locals. In the 18th century it was bought by a Col Wood of Brecon who used part of it as a shooting box when he hunted in the Vale. Then, in 1807, it was bought by Walter Savage Landor, the poet. Landor lived in part of the Priory (the part now occupied by the hotel), but later moved to a house called Siarpol (now a ruin, and seen early in the walk, to the right). The famous poet was as entranced by Ewyas as William de Lacy had been. But instead of religious fervour Landor brought curious agricultural ideas and a reputation for being bad-tempered and argumentative. As well as the Priory building, Landor had acquired the entire Llanthony estate including several farms. The romanticism that made his poetry so popular at that time Landor now applied to these farms. He planted - it is said - 10,000 trees and imported a Spanish species of sheep whose appearance he favoured over the local, hardy mountain sheep. Landor saw the Vale of Ewyas as the ideal setting for a romantic agrarian community, with folk living at one with nature, admiring its beauty and its art and creating their own to complement it. The locals saw him as a dangerous crank, his total ignorance of farming and animal husbandry threatening not only their livelihoods but their lives. As Landor had little difficulty in falling out with people who had no real argument with him - he allegedly fired a pistol at someone at Oxford whose opinions he did not share - he easily managed to be at war with virtually all his tenants and neighbours. In disgust he left the Vale.

Walk Directions   [-] denotes Point of Interest

1. From the car park walk back past the church [1] and down to the valley road, turning right along it. Go past the Half Moon Inn and, after a further 100m, bear right along a track, following it to a gate. Go through, following the path beyond to another gate. Continue straight ahead on the track beyond to Garn Farm.

2. Negotiate the farm by way of gates and maintain direction through more gates to reach 'The Vision' farm. Here, turn left and go through a gate and over a stile before crossing a footbridge over the Afon Honddu. Beyond the bridge the valley road is reached again. Turn right and follow the road to reach a Y-junction at the hamlet of Capel-y-ffin.

3. Take the left-hand fork, soon passing The Monastery [2] on the left.

About 400m from the road fork a path is signed on the left: take this, heading westwards past The Grange to reach a gate. Ahead now a path zig-zags up towards a ridge of the Black Mountains [3]. The climb is gentle at first, then steepens appreciably before easing again as the ridge is approached.

4. The ridge is reached close to a prominent stone known as The Blacksmith's Anvil: turn left here, heading southwards along the gently undulating ridge to reach the triangulation pillar on Bâl Mawr.

5. The path now descends towards the valley, heading gently downhill towards the obvious valley of Cwm Bwchel. At the head of this steep little valley there is a stile: cross this and then another, and go through two gates to reach another footbridge over the Afon Honddu.

6. Continue along the obvious path to reach the valley road again. Cross the road to return to the starting point beside Llanthony Priory [4].

Facilities

There is an inn at Llanthony, and a coffee house in the hotel.

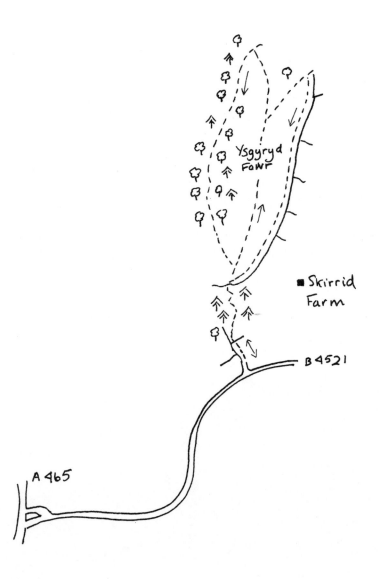

Ysgyryd Fawr

■ Skirrid Farm

B 4521

A 465

Ysgyryd Fawr

OS Maps:	Landranger Sheet 161 (Abergavenny and the Black Mountains)
	Outdoor Leisure Sheet 13 (Brecon Beacons National Park- Eastern Area)
Start:	The car park at Grid Reference 328164, at the southern base of Ysgyryd Fawr.
Access:	The car park lies on the side of the B4521 which leaves the A465 just a little way north of Abergavenny. The car park is to the left of the road about 3 kilometres/2 miles from the main road.
Parking:	Car park beside the B4521.
Grade:	Easy - a little climbing, but short and on good paths.

Points of Interest:

1. Ysgyryd Fawr or Skirrid as the mountain is more commonly known, is a sandstone outlier of the Black Mountains, so well separated from the main mass that despite its relatively low height (486 metres/1,594 feet) it dominates the surrounding area. The smooth, upturned boat profile of the hill is disturbed by a curious cleft about which there are several local legends. One has it that a Jack o'Kent, a wizard in league with the devil (and perhaps a local version of Jack o'Lantern) jumped off Sugar Loaf and caused the cleft with his heel when he landed. Jack o'Kent is also responsible for Harold's Stones (see Walk 1) in one version of their legend.

But the more interesting legends are spiritual in origin. One claims that the cleft opened at the time of the Crucifixion - the Skirrid Arms inn at Llanfihangel Crucorney, to the north of the peak has an inn sign which portrays this event vividly, the hill being struck by lightning. Another legend maintains that the cleft was created by the weight of Noah's Ark landing on the ridge as the flood subsided. As a result of the legends Ysgyryd Fawr was held to be a Holy Mountain and local farmers would sprinkle soil collected from its flanks on to their fields to ensure a good crop. Skirrid soil would also be sprinkled on a coffin during the committal.

The idea of the peak being holy probably accounts for the building of a church on its summit, though the date of the first such church is unknown. The church, dedicated to St Michael, was certainly here before the Reformation as a Mass held each year on Michaelmas was said to draw many hundreds of pilgrims. After the Reformation, Catholicism was outlawed, but the church remained steadfastedly Catholic and drew believers from miles around to secret masses. But the church was too prominent to be a satisfactory venue for services requiring secrecy. It was also too weatherswept to survive without maintenance and, again, too conspicuous for repair work to be carried out. Gradually the church fell into disrepair and then collapsed. Today just a few remnants, and the mounds of earth over old wall bases, remain.

Walk Directions   [-] denotes Point of Interest

1. From the car park head west, towards Abergavenny, soon reaching a signed stile on the right. Cross and follow the path beyond to another stile. Cross this second stile and climb a steep (sometimes stepped) path to reach a wall that marks the boundary of National Trust property. Cross the wall by way of a stone stile and turn right, walking beside the wall for about 80 metres to reach a path going left towards the summit ridge. Follow the ridge to the summit [1].

2. To descend there are three alternatives. The first is to reverse the ascent route. The second is to continue north beyond the summit, descending on a path which soon turns sharp left into fine woodland. Follow the path to reach the stone stile crossed during the ascent. The third alternative takes the eastern flank of the hill: reverse the ascent route for 50 metres, then turn sharply left along a path that descends north-eastwards, then turns sharp right to follow a wall, with splendid views out over the country of the Three Castles, to reach the stone

stile crossed on the ascent.

5. From the stone stile, reverse the outward route back to the car park.

Facilities

None on the route, but there is a full range in Abergavenny, to the west.

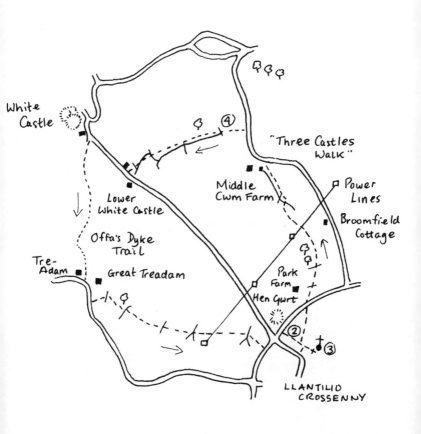

White Castle

④

"Three Castles Walk"

Middle Cwm Farm

Power Lines

Broomfield Cottage

Lower White Castle

Offa's Dyke Trail

Tre-Adam

Great Treadam

Park Farm

Hen Gwrt

②

✝③

LLANTILIO CROSSENNY

52

White Castle

OS Maps:	Landranger Sheet 161 (Abergavenny and the Black Mountains)
	Outdoor Leisure Sheet 13 (Brecon Beacons National Park- Eastern Area)
Start:	White Castle
Access:	White Castle lies a short distance to the south of the B4521 which links the A465 near Abergavenny with the A4137 and A49 near Ross-on-Wye.
Parking:	There is a small car park at White Castle. Limited parking is also available at Llantilio Crossenny church.
Grade:	Moderate - if the 'true' route is taken, route finding is difficult. If not then the route is longer, but easier.

Points of Interest:

1. White Castle is the best preserved of the Three Castles (White, Grosmont and Skenfrith). In its original form it was also the most formidable, perhaps because its position, a few miles further into Gwent than either Grosmont or Skenfrith, meant it needed to be so. For a real appreciation of just how impressive a fortress it was, follow the Offa's Dyke National Trail westward for a short distance. Had the Welsh attacked it is probable that they would have come from the west: White Castle's builders must have made sure that as the Welsh advanced towards it their hearts would sink. White Castle was built in the middle of open country, not close to any town or village, and its design makes it quite clear that this was no fortified manorial hall. At its heart was a massive rectangular keep, brooding over the inner ward which was surrounded by a huge pear-shaped curtain wall (which also enclosed the keep). Outside the curtain wall was a moat. This work was completed, in stone, by the late 12th century - although there was

likely to have been an earlier wooden castle. No further work was carried out until about 1260. The history of White Castle's ownership follows that of Grosmont (see Point of Interest to Walk 9), as the Three Castles were always in common ownership. After the death of Hubert de Burgh the castles were, for about 25 years, in Crown hands, before being passed on to Edmund 'Crouchback', the Earl of Lancaster and Edward I's younger brother. During the time of Crown ownership, Lord Edward - later to be Edward I - took a personal interest in the White Castle. Under his direction, the castle was completely remodelled. Six towers were added to the curtain wall, two of them protecting the gate. The old keep was demolished and an outer ward was added, with its own wall and towers, and its own moat. The resulting castle was the formidable fortress the approaching Welsh would have faced. It is no surprise to learn of Edward's involvement, White Castle is clearly a prelude to the mighty 'Ring of Stone' castles - Conwy, Beaumaris, Caernarfon, Harlech - that he was to throw around Gwynedd.

Unlike Grosmont, White Castle was never attacked - perhaps its appearance acted as a sufficient deterrent, even for Owain Glyndŵr's lieutenant Rhys Gethin. When the age of the castles had passed, it served as a local administration centre. But it was a cold, austere place, remote from civilisation: significant work would have been needed to turn it into a mansion and this was not worthwhile. Instead, White Castle was abandoned - what we see today is what existed in the 16th century, apart from 400 years of decay.

Two last things need mentioning before leaving the castle. The first is - why is it called White? Two theories have been put forward. One asserts that a very early castle on the site was owned by Gwyn ap Gwaethfod and was known as Castell Gwyn. Since *gwyn* is Welsh for 'white', the Anglicisation of the name produced White Castle. The other theory maintains that the external stonework of the castle was given a white plaster coating. There is evidence of white plaster on some of the stonework, but the plastering of castle walls was unusual. Was it another act of intimidation, the formidable castle being whitened to stand out, to glow against the surrounding country?

The second point is a curious incident which took place in 1589 and involves a letter written by a Welshman imprisoned in the Tower of London. The man writes to the Lord Treasurer, Lord Burleigh, regarding White Castle. He recounts a local legend, noting that 'the voyce of the country is that there is a dyvill and his dame, one sets upon a hogshead of gold, the other upon a hogshead of silver' beneath the castle. The man offers his services to Burleigh, wanting to dig beneath the castle. If he finds the treasure and its defending devils, he will 'by the grace of God and without any charge to the Quene or your lordships' throw the pair out and then 'look for something at your hands, for the countrey saith there is a great treasure'. It is a curious tale. Clearly the Welsh prisoner was looking to have himself set free to hunt for the treasure, but he must have either believed the tale or expected Burleigh to believe it. It is, perhaps, another delightful example of the way in which myth and reality intertwine in Wales.

2. Hen Gwrt, the Old Court, is one of the best preserved moated mansion sites in Wales, its moat still water-filled. It is thought that it was constructed in the early 13th century - soon after the building of White Castle. This earliest building was probably a manor house for the lordship of Llantilio Crossenny. The village was then owned by the Bishops of Llandaff, so it is possible that they either installed a landlord or even that the bishops had a country retreat here, moated for security, but close to White Castle for even greater security. A legend that Hen Gwrt was once the home of Dafydd Gam is almost certainly not true.

Excavations have revealed the remains of a building dating from the 14th century on the southern side of the moated square. The 'island' was bridged close to this building, linking it to what is now the B4233. It seems likely that occupation of the site was continuous until the 15th century, but then ceased, possibly because the original house was damaged during the Gwent raids of Owain Glyndŵr's men. After remaining empty for 100 years or so, the island was re-occupied, this time by the masters of Raglan Castle (the Earls of Worcester). The Earls had a deer park locally and built a hunting lodge on the northern side of the island, demolishing what remained of the earlier building and adding a perimeter wall to the island. After a century of occupation the hunting lodge was abandoned and, in 1775, the site was used as a quarry for the construction of Llantilio Court, the hunting lodge and the perimeter wall being demolished. Now just the island - reached by a footbridge - and the moat, presently home to a pair of swans, remain.

3. It is said that close to the River Trothy and the present site of the village of Llantilio Crossenny the Welsh defeated an invading Saxon army. Before the battle, the Welsh had prayed for victory to St Teilo, the 6th century Bishop of Llandaff and in thanks for it they built a church dedicated to the saint. The present church is a replacement for that original, built in the 13th century and with an elegant shingled spire. Inside, the church has several interesting features, particularly the carved corbel heads, one of which is said to be a likeness of Edward II, and a memorial stone inscribed with a portrait of members of 17th century family depicting a man, his wife and three sons, all of them depicted in period costume.

Also in the village is the Hostry Inn. The name is an ancient one, there having been an inn if that name here since at least 1459.

4. The Norman triangle of the Three Castles - Grosmont, Skenfrith and White Castle - are now linked by a Walk of 18 miles/29 kilometres waymarked by a yellow arrow and the words 'Three Castles Walk' on a white border. This walk, and the next two, feature sections of this a fine walk, which explores the interesting county of northern Gwent.

Walk Directions   [-] denotes Point of Interest

The walk follows a section of the Three Castles Walk which is waymarked with a yellow arrow and the words 'Three Castles Walk' on a white background.

1. From the castle [1], go back down the access road to the T-junction. Turn right, passing houses, to the right, to reach a metalled track, on the right. Take this - it is signed as part of the Offa's Dyke National Trail - following it to a T-junction in the hamlet of Tre-Adam. Turn left along the road, passing Great Treadam Farm, then turning next left along a track.

2. Follow the track uphill, with the very beautiful farmhouse, complete with columned porch, on the left. Go through a gate, signed for the Trail, on the right and follow the indistinct path across five fields, linked by well-signed gates/stiles. In the fourth field you pass beneath 400,000 volt power cables.

3. The Trail crosses a final stile on to a road. Turn left, soon passing a road on the right to reach one on the left. The footbridge to Hen Gwrt [2] is a little way along this road. To the right, opposite the road on the left, is a kissing gate: go through and head up the field beyond towards the elbow of a wall. Now follow the wall (it is on your left) through two more kissing gates to reach Llantilio Crossenny church [3].

4. Go back along the outward route to the wall elbow. Now turn half-right and go downhill to reach a gate on to a road. The walker is now faced with a choice. Across the road is a stile beyond which the right of way becomes progressively more difficult to follow as it has been blocked. Those willing to forge a route should have a map and be prepared to use it. The alternative is to go right, then left at the next junction, joining the Three Castles Walk [4] near Broomfield Cottage and following it (and the road) to Middle Cwm Farm.

5. To follow the 'field' route, cross the stile and the field beyond to reach another stile behind the central one of three trees. Cross the next field towards the right corner of a wood. Go through a gate and follow the wood (on your left). Go past a point-to-point (or three-day event) jump, on the left, then use the next jump, also left, to cross a stream. Walk ahead, under the power lines to reach a dog-leg in the far hedge. Follow the hedge to the field corner. Cross the fence (no stile) and turn left to reach a derelict stile. Cross and follow the left edge of the field to its top corner. There, step left to reach the road at Middle Cwm Farm. Turn left.

6. Follow the road to reach a gate (signed for the Three Castles Walk) on the left. Go through a second gate and follow the field edge on the left. In the corner, bear right, then cross a stile on the left. Go over and cross a field to another stile. Now maintain direction to reach a hedge,

following it down to a footbridge. Now head for another footbridge, cross the stile beyond and follow the field edge to another stile. Cross and go down steps to a road. Turn right and follow the road, soon reaching the outward route near the access road for the castle.

Facilities

There is an inn at Llantilio Crossenny.

Skenfrith

OS Maps: Landranger 161 (Abergavenny and the Black Mountains)
              Pathfinder Sheet 1064 {Ross-on-Wye (West)}

Start: Skenfrith Castle

Access: Skenfrith lies on the B4521 which heads south from the
              A49 to the west of Ross-on-Wye.

Parking: There is verge parking at Skenfrith Castle.

Grade: Moderate - field paths and tracks, and some road
              walking.

Points of Interest:

1. Skenfrith is the most romantically sited of the Three Castles, the
waters of the Monnow lapping its walls, but is also the most dour,
with long stretches of high, blank curtain wall with few towers.
Ironically, the Monnow at Skenfrith is not the border between Gwent
and Hereford (and Wales and England), the border ignoring the
dramatic bend the river makes to run close to the village and its
subsequent picturesque meanders in favour of a route that crosses the
hill spur which pushes the river westward.

Skenfrith shares the history of Grosmont and White Castle, but not
its design. Here, in addition to the curtain wall, and a moat on the
sides away from the river, a central round tower was built, a massive
tower capable of independent defence, a last stronghold should the
walls be breached. Though such towers were constructed elsewhere - at
Bronllys and Tretower in nearby Powys for example - it is curious
that the design was used here. The moat and curtain wall were
formidable - why was it felt necessary to back up those defences,
particularly when such a scheme was not employed at Grosmont,
though it must be remembered that at White Castle a rectangular keep,
close to, but not part of, the curtain wall was built. Whatever the

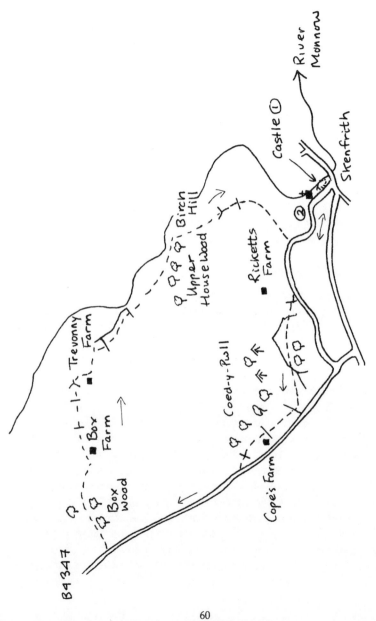

B4347

Box Wood

Box Farm

Trevonny Farm

Birch Hill

Upper House Wood

Coed-y-Prill

Cope's Farm

Ricketts Farm

Castle ①

②

Skenfrith

River Monnow

60

reason it is assumed that the great tower was the main living accommodation for the castle's governor. The living conditions would have been reasonably comfortable, for although lighting was only by way of narrow arrow slits on the ground floor, there were larger windows, and a fireplace, on the upper floors.

Skenfrith did not see action and when peace came to the borderlands after Glyndŵr's rebellion the castle continued to be occupied. Its last known governor died in 1557 and is buried in the village church. The castle was then abandoned and left to decay.

2. This lovely church has a quaint tower which was once a defensive refuge for the villagers and has walls 5ft thick. At its top is a dovecote, a delightful feature. Inside the church is the tomb of John Morgan, the last governor of the Three Castles.

Walk Directions   [-] denotes Point of Interest

The walk follows a section of the Three Castles Walk which is waymarked with a yellow arrow and the words 'Three Castles Walk' on a white background.

1. From the castle [1], follow the village road north-westwards, passing the church [2] and rounding left and right bends to reach a road junction. The return route comes in from the right here: bear left with the road, reaching a track to Ricketts Farm on the right. Just a few steps beyond the track, go up steps on the right and cross a stile.

2. Go half-left across a field to reach a stile and sleeper bridge. Bear half-right to the obvious stile. The right of way bears slightly right in the next field: if it is cropped, turn right, following the field edge, turning left at the corner to continue along a fence to reach a stile across it near the far corner. Bear left, with a copse to the left, to another stile. Maintain direction through a short section of woodland and across a field to a stile. Cross and go down steps, then follow the fence/house on the left. Where the fence ends, bear slightly right to reach a stile and maintain direction to reach another on to a road.

3. Turn right and follow the road to the access road for Box Farm, on

the right. The Three Castles Walk is joined here. Turn right to reach the farm. Go left, between the barns, to reach a gate. Follow the track beyond through a gate to reach Trevonny Farm. Go through a field to reach a gate and continue through two more gates. Now at the next gate do not go through: instead, maintain direction with a fence/hedge on your left. Cross a ditch to reach a stile.

4. Follow the hedge on the left, crossing another stile to reach the farm at Birch Hill. cross two stiles on to the farm drive and bear left along it. The drive becomes surfaced: continue along it to reach the outward route. Turn left and reverse the outward route back to Skenfrith Castle.

Facilities

There is an inn at Skenfrith, on the B4521 close to the castle.

Grosmont

OS Maps:	Landranger 161 (Abergavenny and the Black Mountains) Pathfinder Sheet 1064 {Ross-on-Wye (West)}
Start:	Grosmont Castle
Access:	Grosmont lies on B4347 which links the A465, at Pentrilas, to Rockfield.
Parking:	Parking is straightforward in Grosmont, but please park considerately.
Grade:	Strenuous - field paths and roads, but the route is long and has some climbs.

Points of Interest:

1. The gently country of the valley of the Monnow was a breach in the defences of England from marauding Welshmen. On one side were the Black Mountains, on the other the rugged cliffs of the huge valley and the River Wye itself, broad and deep. But the Monnow Valley was an open door. To the Norman conquerors of England and Gwent it was clear that this breach must be sealed, and to do so they built a triangle of castles, Grosmont, Skenfrith and White Castle, with Grosmont set close to the river at the triangle's northern apex. It is not clear exactly when the first castle was built at Grosmont, but it is likely to have been in about 1150, soon after a Welsh uprising in which the Norman lord of Chepstow was killed. King John recognised the importance of maintaining the Three Castles in single ownership and in 1201 granted them to Herbert de Burgh. Herbert was soon to become one of the most powerful men in England, a guardian to the boy king Henry III and a general whose sea victory over a French fleet off Dover saved the country from invasion. At Grosmont Hubert constructed the castle we now see. The castle is typical of its time, trapezoidal in

GROSMONT

③

②

Castle ①

Little Cross

Cross

Lower Tresenny Farm

River Monnow

Graig Syfyrddin

Cae Robin

White House B4347

Celyn Farm

Brook House Farm

Nant-yr-ych Farm

Duke's Farm

shape with a tower at each corner, a well-fortified gatehouse and a large, rectangular living quarters.

In 1228 Hubert led an expedition against the Welsh, but it was not a success. This, and King Henry's resentment of his guardian's position, led to Hubert's fall from grace. In 1232 he was stripped of the Three Castles. But Hubert had friends among the Marcher lords, and these formed an army determined to restore him to power. Henry was forced to lead an army to Gwent and in early November 1233 he occupied Grosmont. The king stayed at the castle, his army camped outside the walls. As they slept through the night of 11 November, Hubert's friends (perhaps even including a Welsh contingent, with the blessing of Llywelyn the Great) attacked. The King's army was routed, Henry being treated to the sight of many of his senior commanders - lords of his realm - fleeing downhill in their nightshirts and wading across the Monnow to safety. Sensibly, the King made his peace with Hubert and restored the Three Castles to him.

After the death of Llywelyn ap Gruffudd (Llywelyn the Last) in 1282, Wales became more peaceful and the Three Castles lost much of their purpose. Grosmont was now in the hands of the Earls of Lancaster: the son of Earl Henry, also Henry, and known as Henry of Grosmont, was one of the leading generals of the Hundred Years War and was made a Duke by a grateful king. Duke Henry refurbished the castle, turning it from a war engine into a mansion fit for his noble status, but Grosmont's days of conflict were not yet over.

In 1400 Owain Glyndŵr raised his Red Dragon standard of Wales, beginning a rebellion that was to last a dozen years and cost both England and Wales dear. In the early years Glyndŵr was extremely successful, particularly in 1402 when his most able general, Rhys Gethin, won a phenomenal victory at Pilleth. But by 1405 the campaign had become bogged down. Seeking to expand Owain's sphere of influence, which was confined to north and central Wales, Rhys Gethin took an army of 8,000 men southwards. He arrived at Grosmont, attacking it and burning it to the ground. But in the castle was Prince Henry. Born in Monmouth, the prince was to become Henry V, the victor of Agincourt. Perhaps Rhys thought the young prince would be as poor a soldier as his father: perhaps he thought that the prince's Welsh archers would change sides, just as they had at Pilleth. Either way Rhys was sadly mistaken. Prince Henry's men emerged from the castle, putting Rhys' men to flight, then overtaking them and forcing them to fight. Rhys' army was mauled, hundreds being killed and those that survived fleeing in confusion. Such was the scale of the defeat that Glyndŵr was forced to send an army into Gwent immediately, to maintain his credibility and the morale of the Welsh. This new army was led by Owain's brother, Tudur, and his son Gruffudd. They attacked Usk Castle where Prince Henry had now settled his army. Again the prince threw open the castle gates and charged out, scattering the Welsh. On a hill a couple of miles away Tudur and Gruffudd attempted to form a battle line, but Prince Henry arrived before it was finished, smashing the Welsh and pursuing those that fled, hacking them down. Tudur Glyndŵr was killed and Gruffudd was captured, along with several hundred others. Henry executed 300 in front of Usk Castle, but Gruffudd he spared, sending him back to his father as a trophy. Gruffudd was flung into the Tower and left in appalling conditions. He survived for six years before dying of disease.

Grosmont was the beginning of the end for Owain Glyndŵr though the rebellion dragged on for several more years. Of Owain himself nothing certain is known after 1406, nothing at all after 1412. The date of his death, even the year, is unknown and it is not known where he was buried. The Welsh bards maintained that, like Arthur, Owain had taken refuge to await the call to rise and rescue his people. But, intriguingly, there is a legend that Owain spent his twilight years at Kentchurch, just a little way north of Grosmont, on the English side of the river. There, a mystic with magical powers known as John of Kentchurch is said to have been Glyndŵr.

2. St Nicholas' Church is one of the finest in the county. The church was begun in the early 12th century, the spire being added in the 14th. In the 19th century the foundations of the church had to be excavated when it was discovered that the central arches were sinking. It was found that there were springs below the church, and concrete was poured in to stabilise the building. Inside there is a Norman font and a fine effigy of a knight, probably dating from the 14th century.

3. Grosmont is a delightful place, half hidden in the folds of gently undulating country close to a lazy meander of the River Monnow which forms the border between Gwent and Hereford - Wales and England. Medieval Grosmont was an important market town, but it never recovered from the ravages of Rhys Gethin - Owain Glyndŵr's lieutenant. Camden the Elizabethan traveller, claimed to have been able to see the lines of old streets destroyed by Rhys, but little remains now of Grosmont's former importance, apart from the town church.

Walk Directions   [-] denotes Point of Interest

The walk follows a section of the Three Castles Walk which is waymarked with a yellow arrow and the words 'Three Castles Walk' on a white background.

1. From the Grosmont castle [1], follow the B4347 (Skenfrith) road downhill, crossing a tributary stream of the Monnow. Go past Lower Tresenny Farm (right), then go over a signed stile on the right, next to a gate. Follow the track beyond to another stile, cross and walk along the right edge of a field to reach a stile. Follow the left edge of the next field to a footbridge.

2. There are steps beyond the bridge. Do not climb these: instead, go left through trees and follow the edge of the field beyond to reach a track, following it past a barn. Now bear right up steps, cross a stile and bear left past a cottage.

3. Turn right, cross a field to a stile and maintain direction to reach another stile. The next stile is in the top left corner of the next field. Cross and go left, uphill, to the corner of the woodland. The waymarking is excellent for the next part of the walk, which is just as well as the route finding through the trees is complex: follow a track uphill, go over a stile and continue through the wood, exiting over a stile.

4. Walk beside a fence (with it on your right), then turn left to reach a stile. Continue (with a fence now on your left), following a track

downhill to reach a track junction. Turn right, downhill, then left at the next junction to reach a stile. Cross and walk with a fence on your right, but where it bends away, maintain direction to reach a stile. Cross and follow the fence on the right to reach a track: now follow the track to a stile.

5. Go over the stile and continue (fence on left) to reach a gate. Do not go through: instead, turn right to reach a stile. Now maintain direction to reach a fence and follow it to a stile on to a road near White House.

6. The Three Castles Walk turns left here, but we turn right, following the road steeply down past Brook House Farm (left) to cross a stream. Beyond, a short-cut is possible along a footpath to the right. However, this is unmarked and the land is marked as private woodland. It is possible to follow the right of way - go through the gate and follow the track beyond, bearing left, uphill to Cae Robin and following the track to a road - but is only recommended to experienced map readers with a taste for adventure. The best way is to continue along the road, passing the delightful Nant-yr-ych Farm (right) and Duke's Farm (also on the right) to reach a crossroads.

7. Turn sharp right up a road marked as a 'No Through Road'. This road climbs steadily with wonderful views to the right (east) across the Monnow valley. Tree-topped May Hill and the solid wall of the Cotswolds can be seen in the distance.

8. Beyond Celyn Farm (right) barns are reached on the left. To the right here is the track which brings the short-cut right of way: it, too, is unmarked. Continue along the road to rejoin the Three Castle Walk (which comes in from the left at Graig Farm Wood.)

9. Continue along the road to reach a signed stile beside a gate. Cross the stile and follow the track beyond downhill, with a wonderful view of Grosmont ahead. Follow the track through several gates. The track becomes surfaced: continue along it to the bottom of the valley. There, turn left over a footbridge and follow a track steeply uphill to reach a road. Turn left, passing the church [2] to return to Grosmont [3].

Facilities

There is a full range of facilities in the village.

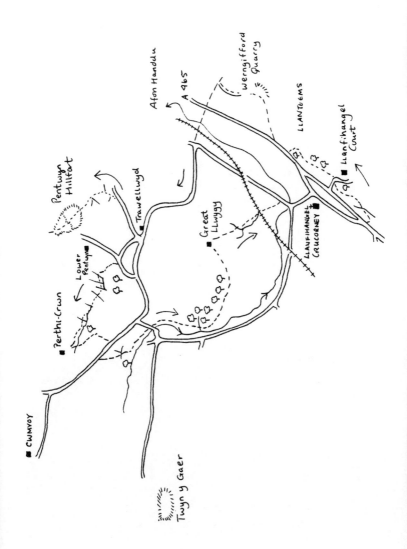

CWMYOY

Pentwyn Hillfort

Perthi-Crwn

Lower Pentwyn

Trawelhwyd

Great Llwygy

Twyn y Gaer

Afon Honddu

A 465

Wernyifford Quarry

LLANTEEMS

LLANFIHANGEL CRUCORNEY

Llanfihangel Court

Llanfihangel Crucorney

OS Maps: Landranger Sheet 161 (Abergavenny and the Black Mountains)
Outdoor Leisure Sheet 13 (Brecon Beacons National Park- Eastern Area)

Start: Llanfihangel Crucorney

Access: Llanfihangel Crucorney is bypassed by the A465, Abergavenny to Hereford road. Heading north from the roundabout south of Abergavenny the village is reached, on the left, after about 4¹/₂ miles.

Parking: There is a rough parking area at the northern end of the village, by the village stores (where a small charge is payable). Parking is also possible, with permission, at the Skirrid Inn and, with care, elsewhere in the village.

Grade: Moderate - mostly field paths, but with a surprising amount of climbing. The main A465 also has to be crossed twice which requires great care.

Points of Interest:

1. Llanfihangel's Skirrid Inn is claimed to be not only the oldest in Gwent, but the oldest in Wales. Certainly some parts of the main fabric date from around 1100 and many of the windows, and the front door, are medieval. Inside there are magnificent beamed ceilings: it is claimed that some of these beams were once the masts of sailing ships trading at Newport and Chepstow. On a less happy note it is also claimed that the large beam over the stair well was once used as a gallows. After the Duke of Monmouth's rebellion failed at the Battle of Sedgemoor on 6 July 1685 Judge Jeffreys was appointed to try and sentence those who had (or were said to have) supported the Duke. Jeffreys' Bloody Assizes were mostly held in England's west country -

Dorset and Somerset - but the Welsh borders were not spared. Victims of the Bloody Assizes included several who met their end below the Skirrid Inn's beam. The inn's sign is a splendid illustration of the creation of Skirrid Mountain's cleft (see Walk 6).

The village church, dedicated to St Michael, is a fine 13th century building now, sadly, half open to the elements.

2. The Court is a beautiful multi-gabled Elizabethan house built by Rhys Morgan (though he actually remodelled an existing house.) There are marvellous stone stairs leading to the front (north) entrance and equally good windows on the east side. The Earl of Worcester, who owned the Court after Morgan, added stables in fine Jacobean style. Tradition maintains that Charles II slept at the Court in 1645 and one room - with a magnificent cross-beamed ceiling - is named for him. The tradition seems to be well-founded as Charles certainly spent the night of 1 July in Abergavenny and that of 3 July in Raglan. The Court is occasionally open to the public in the summer.

3. Pen-twyn is an Iron Age hillfort, an early form of such fort, as it has only a single rampart and ditch. Later forms - necessitated by the invention of the sling which allowed attackers to bombard the defenders from outside the defences - had multiple ditches and ramparts. Pen-twyn is also of the type known as a promontory fort as it occupies the end of a ridge rather than a summit. The rectangular fort is divided into two sections by an east-west running bank with a ditch on its southern side, suggesting that the first fort was only the northern part of what we see, and was expanded at a later stage when the southernmost defences were added. At the south-eastern corner of the fort, close to where the route enters it, there is the original entrance. It is an elaborate series of ramparts built to turn an attacker's right (unshielded) side to the defenders.

Despite the fact that most hill forts are seen as defensive structures for a particular community, some experts believe that the presence of another fort, Twyn y Gaer, on the ridge to the west, implies that the pair protected the Honddu valley in the way of later castles. This would mean that Pen-twyn was a military engine rather than purely a defensive structure.

4. St Martin's Church, Cwmyoy is an extraordinary building, there being not one square joint (wall or roof) in it. This curiosity cannot be laid at the door of incompetent builders, however, but on the nature of the ground on which it stands - though why a flatter spot was not chosen is far from clear. The church is medieval and is also remarkable for the history of its fine medieval cross. This may have been originally placed in the church, but was found in the 19th century in a field close to the village. Had it been hidden during the Puritan purges and then forgotten? Restored to the church it was St Martin's greatest treasure until 1967 when it was stolen. The church officials showed a photograph of the cross to experts at the British Museum - as a prelude to issuing a description. The expert dated it to the 13th century, but then recalled that he had seen it just a few days before at a local antique shop. The cross was recovered and returned to the church.

Cwmyoy is not the only worthwhile local church for walkers to visit. Partrishow on the other side of the Honddu Valley is also medieval and houses several treasures. The church was built on the site of the hermitage cell of St Ishow who was murdered by robbers. Inside there is a 'doom figure' - Father Time depicted as a skeleton holding a dagger, a spade and an hour glass. This extremely rare mural is on the wall near the door - placed there so that the congregation would see it on their way out and remember that life was short and should be lived in a godly way to ensure an easy path to heaven. The church also has a superb medieval carved rood screen. These screens held a cross (the rood), but also performed the useful function of preventing the congregation's dogs from fouling the altar.

Walk Directions   [-] denotes Point of Interest

1. From the village, walk south-westwards along the road to return to the A465, passing the Skirrid Inn and church [1], and a couple of lovely buildings - Gwent Lodge, to the left, and the Old Vicarage on the right. Cross the main road, with great care, and go up the metalled path to the right of the bus stop.

2. The path soon reaches a road. Almost immediately go left over a

stile and head across the field beyond. When a ditch/fence comes into view, head for this and follow it to a footbridge over the ditch. Cross and turn left. Cross a stile and continue to a road.

3. Turn right. Llanfihangel Crucorney Court [2] is ahead. After 15 yards (where the road goes sharp right), turn left along a broad track. The track soon follows a fence, on the right. Where this ends, maintain direction, now with an orchard on the right. There is a stream on the left: where this is bridged, step left across the bridge and turn right to walk with the stream on your right. The right of way actually crosses the orchard on the left, but the reasonable route follows the stream to the orchard's end, then goes up and left around the edge to reach a stile and steps down to the main road.

4. Turn right and follow the broad verge, crossing a road and, soon, reaching signed steps on the right. Climb these and go half-left towards a raised embankment between trees. This is the track bed of an old railway which served the local stone quarries.

5. Follow the embankment - at one point, where a bridge has been demolished you go left, steeply downhill (the descent is partially stepped) over a footbridge and steeply up again - with good views of Skirrid Mountain to the right. The embankment curves around houses, to the left, to reach a stile on to a lane. Go left, but soon right over a stile. Follow the fence on the left, crossing a stile/footbridge, then turning right, and then left with the fence to reach a stile on the left.

6. You have now joined the Offa's Dyke National Trail. Cross the stile and follow the Trail to the A465. Cross the road, again with great care, and follow the lane opposite, soon turning left over a stile. (The Lancaster Arms Inn is to the right.) Follow the Trail to reach, and cross, the Afon Honddu and the railway, the latter with care.

7. Cross a stile on to a road and walk ahead. Look to the left here to see a conspicuous mound, the remains of an ancient castle motte. Just beyond the motte and Treveddw Farm, go over a signposted stile on the right and head towards a mast. On rejoining the road, bear right and follow it to a junction at Trawellwyd. Turn right, still following

the Offa's Dyke Trail, going downhill to reach a track on the left. Follow the Trail along this track, going uphill to reach the Pen-twyn hill fort [3].

8. Now leave the Trail, bearing left across the hill fort to reach a track. Turn left and follow this track south-westwards, passing Lower Pen-twyn. Go past a track junction, on the left, then turn right over a stile. Bear slightly right, downhill and cross another stile. Now maintain direction, going downhill more steeply to cross a stream and a stile.

9. Bear left, uphill, to reach a fence. Turn right with the fence and cross a stream and a stile. Follow the fence on the left, going through a gate and, further on, crossing a stile. There is a superb view of Cwmyoy church [4] from here.

10. Just before reaching Perthi-Crwn Farm, go left, following a fence to a gate. Follow the track beyond, going through another gate. Follow an enclosed track, then bear right in a field to reach a gate on to a road, with Pont Rhys Powell Farm to the left.

11. Turn right, but after about 125 metres go left over a stile. Go diagonally across the field beyond to reach a stream and a gate. Maintain direction across a field, crossing a footbridge and then following the Afon Honddu to Pont Rhys Powell. A detour here visits the Twyn y Gaer hill fort: turn right along the road to its junction by the Queen's Head Inn follow the track opposite, then break left to the hill top fort. If the detour is followed you must return to the bridge along the same route.

12. Cross the road and a stile, and continue beside the river. Cross a footbridge, then leave the river (which bears away right), heading across a field to reach a footbridge and stile. Now follow the river again to reach a footbridge over it. Do not cross: instead, bear left (stepping stones) into Strawberry Wood, a small nature reserve. Climb up through the wood, crossing a stile, going through a small gate and crossing another stile. Walk with a fence on your right to reach another stile.

13. Follow the edge of a field, cross a stile and bear left towards Great

Llwygy Farm. There, cross a stile, go between the barns, turn right by the house, then right again over a stile and bear left across the field beyond to another stile and plank bridge. Follow the hedge on the right, cross a stile and walk down to another on the right.

14. Cross the railway, with great care, and follow a path which soon rejoins the Afon Honddu. At the road, turn right, then left at the junction to return to the start.

Facilities

There is an inn and a general store at Llanfihangel-Crucorney.

Raglan

OS Maps: Landranger 161 (Abergavenny and the Black Mountains)
              Outdoor Leisure Sheet 14 (Wye Valley and Forest
              of Dean)

Start: Raglan Church

Access: Raglan lies close to the junction of the A449 dual
              carriageway heading north from the M4 near Caerleon
              and the A40 Monmouth to Abergavenny dual
              carriageway. There is a slip road off the A40 just to the
              west of the junction and an exit to the town from a
              roundabout a little further west.

Parking: There is street parking in Raglan, particularly in Castle
              Street opposite the church.

Grade: Easy - with field paths throughout, but the route crosses
              the busy A40 twice.

Points of Interest:

1. Raglan church is dedicated to St Cadog, a 6th century Celtic saint
with no known connection to the town. There is a legend that St
David did spend time at Raglan, and at that an earlier church was
dedicated to him, but no real evidence for this exists. The present
church dates, in part, from the 14th century, with 15th century
additions following a bequest in the will of William Herbert, the 1st
Earl of Pembroke. The church was damaged during the Civil War
siege, restored, and then restored again in the mid-19th century. The
clock in the tower was the gift of a local woman, Anna Maria
Bosanquet. It is said that she demanded that the church bells be
removed as they were too noisy, but gave the clock and its faces to
make amends. In the churchyard is the base of a 15th century
preaching cross.

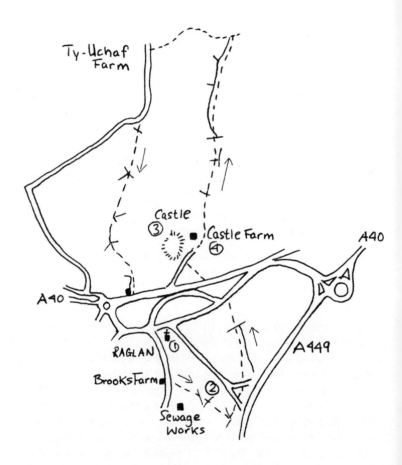

Ty-Uchaf Farm

Castle

③

Castle Farm

④

A40

A40

RAGLAN

Brooks Farm

①

②

A449

Sewage Works

2. The fields here are known as Leaguer Fields and were used by the Parliamentarian army which besieged Raglan in 1646. The dead from that campaign were buried in a field to the west of the castle, still called Gwaelod-y-Beddau, the Meadow of Graves.

3. It is not known with certainty when the first castle was built at Raglan. Soon after the Norman conquest a string of castles were placed on the border between Norman England and the Welsh, castles at Chepstow, Monmouth, Caerleon and Abergavenny. It is possible that there was one at Raglan too, and there was certainly one by 1174 when Richard Strongbow of Chepstow granted it to Walter Bloet. Eventually the castle passed to a Welshman, William ap Thomas, who had served the English Crown in France and was married to Gwladys the daughter of Sir Dafydd Gam. Gam - Dafydd ap Llywelyn ap Hywel to give him his Welsh name: his English 'surname' means crooked, because he had a squint - is one of Wales' most curious figures. He was long-armed, red-haired and quick tempered. It is said he left his home town of Brecon when still very young after killing a man in a rage. Dafydd joined the service of John of Gaunt and there he became a friend of Henry Bolingbroke, later Henry IV. In 1404 at the height of his power in Wales, Owain Glyndŵr held his famous parliament in Machynlleth. At it, Dafydd Gam attempted to kill him, an extraordinary act for a Welshman. It is thought that Gam was acting as an agent for Bolingbroke. Glyndŵr was not renowned for acts of mercy, but he had Gam imprisoned rather than executed. When Glyndŵr disappeared Gam was released and went to France with Henry V. At the Battle of Agincourt it is famously told that the king, looking across at the French army, asked Dafydd how many French he thought there were. 'Enough to kill, to take prisoner and to run away', Dafydd replied. During the battle Dafydd saved the king's life by intercepting a blow meant for him. As he lay dying he was knighted by the king. It is believed that Shakespeare's Fluellen, his all-purpose Welshman, was modelled on Gam which, if true, is a great irony.

Dafydd Gam may never have visited Raglan, but he would have been proud of his grandson, who was born there. Sir William Herbert became the 1st Earl of Pembroke, the first Welshman to be ennobled by the English throne. As Pembroke he commanded the Yorkist army at the Battle of Edgecote in July 1469, but he had inherited his grandfather's temper. On the night before the battle he ordered Lord Stafford, his second-in-command, out of the inn they were sharing. Stafford was outraged, the more so because, as a contemporary account has it, 'he delighted muche to be for the love of a damassle that dwelled in the house'. As the armies faced each other, Stafford turned his men around and marched away. The Yorkists lost and Pembroke, caught at the door of a church he was attempting to enter in order to gain sanctuary, was beheaded.

William ap Thomas and his son were responsible for most of the Raglan castle we now see. It was William who built the formidable Great Tower, a vast hexagonal structure known as the Twr Melyn (Yellow Tower) of Gwent. The tower was built in the early 15th century, but even in the 17th century it was said that 'for height, strength and neatness, it surpasses most, if not every other tower of England and Wales'. Lord Pembroke carried on the tradition of his father, building superb additions to the castle, all in the finest stonework and including some of Wales' earliest brickwork. Pembroke added the Pitched Stone and Fountain Courts, the latter with a marble fountain at its centre from which clear water ran continually.

The castle eventually passed to Charles Somerset who was created Earl of Worcester in 1514. A later Earl was still in possession of the castle when the Civil War broke out. But at this point it is worth mentioning a curious episode relating to the Earl's son, Lord Herbert. He had apparently invented a machine that raised water very quickly. No details of his device are known with certainty, but it was obviously real rather than a trick, used water as its driving force and made a great deal of noise - one group of locals was frightened half to death by the machine, the more so when they were told the noise was being made by escaped lions. What was it? There has been speculation that Herbert had been experimenting with steam drive, and with some success, but nothing can be proved.

On 14 June 1645 the Royalists were defeated at Naseby and Charles I rode west to stay at Raglan, the home of the loyal Lord Worcester. The king stayed for 3 weeks and returned in September.

The following year, on 3 June, a Parliamentarian army arrived at Raglan and called on Worcester to surrender. Worcester was by now 85 years old, but his response was uncompromising - 'I make choice, if it so please God, to die nobly than to live in infamy'. The castle was encircled, Parliamentarian reinforcements arriving after the fall of Oxford. In August Sir Thomas Fairfax arrived in August and took over negotiations himself. By 17 August it was clear to Worcester that Fairfax's men had all but undermined the defences and were bound to succeed.

Raglan was surrendered on 19 August. Worcester was taken to the Tower, but a compassionate Parliament decided to move him to Windsor Castle. On being told Worcester is said to have cried out 'God bless my soul, they will give me a grander castle than they took away'. But it was not to be, the old man dying in the Tower before being moved.

At Raglan, the fearful Parliamentarians decided to ensure that never again would the castle threaten them. They bombarded it with cannon, but to no avail, so locals were called and with pickaxes they undermined the walls, shoring them up with wooden props which were then set alight. The castle's defences, including the Great Tower, collapsed, creating the ruin we see today.

4. Castle Farm was built in the 17th century by the 5th Earl of Worcester. It is built of red Raglan brick.

Walk Directions   [-] denotes Point of Interest

1. From the church [1], follow the minor road (Chepstow Road) towards Devauden and Chepstow, ignoring the footpath, on the left, after the school. Just before Brooks Farm, on the right, and after passing a brick building, on the left, go through a gate on the right and follow a track towards the sewage works.

2. Bear left over a concrete bridge and maintain direction to reach a gate. Go diagonally across the field [2] beyond to the far left corner. Cross a stile and sleeper bridge and bear slightly left, following the edge of a rugby pitch to reach a gate on to a lane.

3. Cross the lane, go through a gate and maintain direction uphill across a paddock to reach a stile behind a shed. Cross on to a lane and go over the signed stile opposite. Head towards the finest of the fine trees ahead, then follow the hedge on the right, crossing a stile, to reach a stile on to a road. The right of way is now ahead, up the drive of 'Kamdoh' and along the left edge of its lawn: there is actually a derelict stile beyond the cypress hedge at the far side of the lawn. But to avoid this gross invasion of privacy, go right, following the road to the main A40.

4. Turn left, following the wide verge, then crossing, with great care, to reach a signed path opposite. Go down steps, over a stile and up the field beyond to reach a gate on to a lane. Opposite is the car park for Raglan Castle [3], an alternative start.

5. Turn right to Castle Farm [4] and cross a signed stile by a gate. Cross another stile to the right of a barn, and yet another a little further on, over the fence on the left. Turn right, then left over a stile and left again over another.

6. Cross a track and a stile and bear right across the field beyond. Go over a stile and continue, going through the left-hand, barred, gate and on to another stile. Cross this and follow the field edge uphill to reach a stile on the right. Go over and turn left along a bridleway.

7. When the bridleway reaches a road, turn left, passing Ty Uchaf Farm to reach a distinct right bend. Here, go through the gate on the left and bear right (as signed). Now maintain direction across two fields - there is a gate at the first fence, but at the second, where three hedges meet, there is, at present no stile.

8. Beyond, head for the right end of the hedge ahead, then bear left through an arch in a hedge and bear left again across the next field to reach a hedge corner. Now follow the hedge/houses on the right to reach a stile on to the A40. It is (relatively) easy to cross here, as traffic from the right is accelerating away from the roundabout and that from the left is slowing into the roundabout. Nevertheless, take great care. On the far side, turn left along the wide verge to reach a gap in the wall on the right.

9. Go through and turn right, crossing a hump-backed bridge into Castle Street, Raglan. Follow this street to return to the church.

Facilities

There is a full range of facilities in the town.

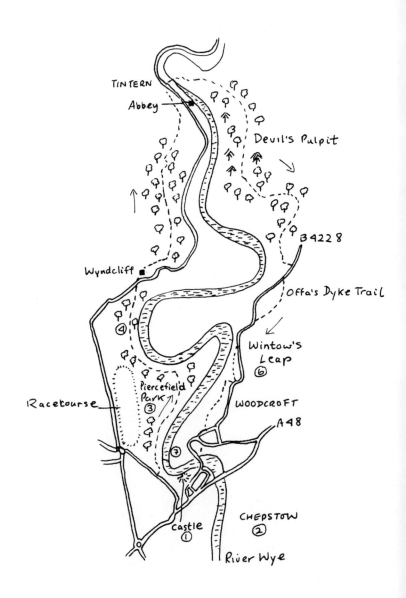

TINTERN

Abbey

Devil's Pulpit

B 4228

Wyndcliff

Offa's Dyke Trail

④

Wintow's Leap
⑥

Racecourse

Piercefield Park
③

WOODCROFT

A 48

⑦

castle
①

CHEPSTOW
②

River Wye

Walk 12

6 miles/9½ kilometres
or 13 miles/21 kilometres

Chepstow

OS Maps: Landranger Sheet 162 (Gloucester and Forest of Dean)
Outdoor Leisure Sheet 14 (Wye Valley and Forest
of Dean)

Start: Chepstow Castle

Access: Chepstow lies on the A48 which runs close to the
western shore of the River Severn, and close to the
A466 Wye Valley road. It is a short distance from the
M48.

Parking: There is a car park at Chepstow Castle and another in
the centre of town. There is also limited (and time-
limited), street parking.

Grade: Moderate - Woodland and field paths, but with some
climbing. If the complete route is walked, the grade is
strenuous as the walk is long. However there are
excellent refreshment facilities at the half-way point.

Points of Interest:

1. The first castle was built by William FitzOsbern, one of William
the Conqueror's chief advisers, in 1067, though it was much extended
and restored later. It has had an eventful history: it acted as a prison for
Edward II before he was taken to Berkeley and murdered, and for the
father-in-law of Edward IV before he was taken to Kenilworth
for execution. In the second Civil War, of 1648, the castle was
captured and held for the Royalists by Sir Nicholas Kemeys. The
threat this posed was enough to bring Cromwell to the scene and the
castle was badly damaged by cannon fire. Sir Nicholas had left boats
as a means of escape, tied up at the foot of the castle wall, but a
Parliamentary soldier swam the river and cut them free to drift away.

After that the castle wall was breached and many Royalists ran out to surrender. The rest, including Kemeys, stayed. They were all killed, a plaque marking the spot of Kemeys' death.

After the war ended, the castle was soon in use (again) as a prison, this time for Sir Henry Marten. Marten had been one of those who signed the death warrant for Charles I, suggesting that the signatories 'should serve His Majesty as the English did his Scottish grandmother, and cut off his head'. Later he refused to agree to Cromwell accepting the crown (he was at least consistent) but was imprisoned for life after the Restoration. He was imprisoned in Marten's Tower, but his life seems to have been pleasant enough: he was allowed friends and often went out to dinner. At the age of 78 Marten died: he is buried in the town church under a slab bearing indifferent lines of verse, the main purpose of which were to spell out HENRY MARTEN with the first letter of each line.

2. The name Chepstow is Saxon for a market town, the Saxon word *ceping* for market having survived often, even at Cheapside in London. As a market town, Chepstow has always been relatively prosperous, though it was not always wholesome: in 1804 the parish accounts note that Thomas King, the town crier, was paid 1 shilling for 'Crying Piggs not to be suffered about the Streets', and later the market sold opium and leeches openly. It is a fine town, worthy of time to explore. The town walls and the superb town gate were built in the 14th century. The gate is not original, having been almost entirely rebuilt in the early 1500s and renovated at times since.

3. Piercefield Park, now the home of Chepstow Racecourse, was once the home of Valentine Morris. Morris seems to have been a likeable spendthrift: he succeeded to a fortune when his father died, including property in Antigua, and determined to create at Piercefield a paradise on earth. He employed a landscape architect to assist him, and together they laid out a series of walks between ten viewpoints. Each viewpoint was fancifully named - the Chinese Seat, the Druid's Temple - and equipped. The Grotto, for instance, was a cave hollowed from solid rock and filled with copper and iron cinders. At each viewpoint there were seats so that the visitor could take in the view.

Morris also entertained lavishly and, ultimately, added gambling to his list of vices. Eventually in 1770, when giant ants attacked his Antiguan plantations and they made no profit for the year, he went bankrupt and had to sell the Park. When he departed from Chepstow for Antigua the church bell was muffled and rung, and a sorrowing crowd lined the streets. Morris was so touched that he cried. He did well in the West Indies and was appointed Lieutenant Governor of St Vincent. At his own expense he prepared the islands for defence against the French but lost everything when the French invaded. The pain of this second bankruptcy drove his wife insane and Morris was imprisoned for debt in England despite the fact that the government owed him more than the total of his debts. It was a sad case of bureaucratic bungling, but it was never resolved and Morris died in poverty.

Close to the Wye in the Park a local proverb was enacted, for it was said that the man born to hang will not drown. Thomas Moxley was on his way to Chepstow one night 'somewhat disguised with liquor' (what a wonderful phrase!) when he fell off a cliff and down towards the river. He broke a leg and was badly injured but survived drowning as the tide was going down, leaving the bushes in which he landed high and dry. Unable to move, Moxley lay waiting for the next tide to engulf him, but his groans were heard by fishermen riding the tide, and they rescued him. He recovered well and two years later stole a horse - for which he was hanged at Monmouth Jail.

4. The woodland here was famed as a poaching ground and produced some great characters who brought colour to the local scene. One famous local walked stiff-legged at all times to try to disguise the times when he did it because he had to, a gun barrel being pushed down each trouser leg. Ultimately he was caught for pheasant shooting. His defence was straightforward: 'Indeed your honour I never shot no pheasants at all. The only bird I shot was a rabbit, and I knocked that down with a stick'.

The woods and river could be hazardous though, especially if the traveller was a little unsteady. One unfortunate started shouting 'Man lost!' when he became hopelessly entangled and panic-stricken. An owl answered 'Whoo-whoo' and he yelled back that it was the clockmaker from Chepstow.

5. The top of the Wyndcliff is 700 foot above the river, though not all of that height is climbed by the 365 steps laid out in 1828 by staff of the Duke of Beaufort who owned much land around here, including Tintern Abbey. Recent repair work has reduced the number to around 300.

6. The cliff is name for Sir John Wintour, a Royalist sympathiser in the Civil War. Wintour fortified his own mansion at Lydney, though he was away when a Roundhead army called. He need not have worried, for his wife defended the house so strongly that the Parliamentarians wearily retreated. Sir John was anxious that the cliffs near Beachley should be fortified, the Severn at that point being easily crossed by barge. He was about this business when his group was surprised by a contingent of Roundheads under Colonel Massey. The Royalists were heavily defeated, some, including Wintour, scrambling down the Sedbury cliffs to the safety of boats. This escape is likely to have given rise to the legend of Wintour's Leap, with Sir John leaping down the shallow Beachley cliffs on horseback. A later action, near Lancaut, also saw Wintour involved in a last-minute retreat and it is probable that it was this event that gave rise to the naming of the cliffs, with the horseback leap being transferred here in popular imagination. It is, after all, unlikely that Sir John leapt down these cliffs, in one go or several, and survived.

7. The tidal effects of the Wye at Chepstow have caused some extensive flooding, the river once rising seventy feet in one tide, and once coming up so fast that a woman and girl were drowned in bed. But it is more renowned at this point for being the grave of 'evidence' that Francis Bacon wrote Shakespeare's plays. The supposed evidence was a complete set of manuscripts in Bacon's hand, plus supporting notes telling the story of why he had persuaded an unknown Stratford actor to accept responsibility for them. Their whereabouts had been 'discovered' by Dr Orville Owen of Detroit, who had, he said, unravelled clues left by Bacon. Dr Owen arrived in Chepstow in 1909, first searching a cave near the castle, then building a coffer dam in the

river to search the bed. The good doctor eventually retreated empty-handed.

Walk Directions   [-] denotes Point of Interest

The directions below are for the full route, but the walk can easily be broken into two fine linear routes, finishing (or starting) at Tintern. Tintern is linked to Chepstow by an excellent bus service operated by Stagecoach, running every 2 hours from Monday to Saturday.

1. From Chepstow Castle [1] go out on to Bridge Street and turn right, climbing towards the town centre. Go ahead when the road bears left, to reach Beaufort Square [2]. Go diagonally left across the square then right into High Street. Go through the Town Gate and turn right along Welsh Street.

2. Turn right (as signed for the Wye Valley Walk) along the 'No Entry' road - the exit from the Leisure Centre car park - crossing the car park to reach an information board on the Walk. Bear left and follow the well-signed and well-trodden Walk through the wood of Piercefield Park [3]. Soon, a wall is reached: go over the stile which crosses it and continue through the wood [4]. The path performs a sweeping left-hand turn, approaching the River Wye. The river is at the base of the steep ground on the right, but is only visible, fleetingly, in winter when the leaves have fallen. On the left is Chepstow Racecourse.

3. The path is climbing gently now. Beyond the racecourse it climbs more steeply, at one point using steps, to reach a car park at the edge of the A466. Cross the road, with great care, and take the signed track opposite, crossing a car barrier. Follow the waymarked route through the beautiful Wyndcliffe woodland to reach the bottom of the 365 steps [5]. From the top of the steps follow the waymarked route (this is still the Wye Valley Walk) which undulates gently through woodland. A stile is crossed before the route descends steeply through a tight valley to reach the A466 at Tintern.

5. To return to Chepstow, cross the main road, with great care, and follow Walk 4 to the Devil's Pulpit and on to the point where Walk 4

leaves the Offa's Dyke National Trail.

6. Now continue along the Offa's Dyke Trail, following a wall through Boatswood Plantation and then descending steps. Continue through woodland, crossing a stile and following the path beyond to reach the B4228. Turn right and follow the road, with care, for 800 metres to reach a signed path (for the Offa's Dyke Trail) on the left.

7. Follow the path across open land, then through Wallhope Grove to reach a stone stile. Go over on to the B4228. Turn left and follow the road, again with care, for 500 metres, going around a left-hand bend from where there is a fine view of Wintour's Leap [6] and the huge meander of the River Wye. 150 metres beyond the bend, go right along a signed path behind the houses of Woodcroft village, regaining the B4228 after 700 metres.

8. Bear right, but, soon, go right, again, following the Offa's Dyke Trail to reach a section of the real dyke. When the path reaches the B4228 again, turn right and follow it to the A48.

9. Cross, with great care, and go down the lane opposite. Soon, the Offa's Dyke National Trail goes left. Do not follow it: instead, continue ahead to rejoin the A48 opposite the very elegant, but very narrow, bridge across the Wye [7]. There is a wonderful view of Chepstow Castle from here. Cross the bridge, with great care, and continue ahead (Bridge Street) to reach the castle, on the right.

Facilities

There is a full range of facilities in Chepstow.

Walk 13

Risca

OS Maps:	Landranger Sheet 171 (Cardiff, Newport and surrounding area) Pathfinder Sheet 1130 (Cwmbrân)
Start:	Darren Road, Risca (GR 235 914)
Access:	Risca lies to the north of the A467 Newport to Newbridge road and is reached by a road from a roundabout on that main road.
Parking:	Parking is possible, with consideration, near Darren Road. It is easier at St Mary's Church, but this adds 1¹/₄ miles (2 kilometres) to the walk.
Grade:	Moderate - Although the walking is straightforward, on tracks and paths, there is a considerable amount of climbing.

Points of Interest:

1. The Twmbarlwm fort is of great interest, paradoxically because it is not clear when it was first constructed. At its eastern edge there is a large, conical, flat-topped mound, clearly the motte of a Norman motte and bailey castle. The motte has a defensive ditch around its base, and on the western side of this ditch, at its very edge, is a Bronze Age cairn burial. The bailey section of the castle is, as usual, surrounded by a ditch and rampart, but this is not complete, having significant gaps in its western and southern points. As it is known that Twmbarlwm had a Bronze Age presence, it is possible that there was an Iron Age hill fort here, though the missing sections of defences do not support that idea: the Iron Age folk would not have left such an inviting gap, and there is no evidence of gateways at the missing sections. Many historians therefore believe that the Twmbarlwm site is entirely medieval (apart from the Bronze Age burial). If that is so,

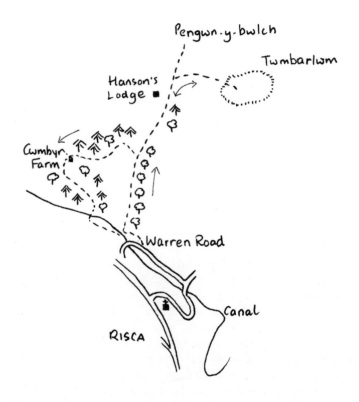

Pengwn·y·bwlch

Twmbarlwm

Hanson's Lodge

Cwmbyr Farm

Warren Road

Canal

RISCA

the fort shows a remarkable consistency of design and method over a period of several thousand years.

The likely builder of the Twmbarlwm motte and bailey is Gilbert de Clare, the local Norman lord in the latter part of the 13th century. De Clare was an expansionist, seeking to increase his land-holding by pushing westwards, a move that had brought him into direct conflict with Llywelyn ap Gruffudd over the ownership of Senghenydd. Twmbarlwm may have been involved in that conflict.

2. The Monmouthshire and Brecon Canal seen - but briefly and from a distance - on Walk 14, was authorised by an Act of Parliament (as required by all canals) in 1793. It was dug by hand - as were all the canals - a remarkable memorial to muscle power. The digging has also given us our (now slang) expression for manual workers. The men who dug the canals, or navigations as they were then called (hence the name of the nearby road), were known as navigators, or 'navvies' for short. The Risca arm of the canal, which was eventually extended beyond Pontypool to Newport, met the Abergavenny arm close to Newport and served the expanding coal and brick industries of Risca.

3. Although Risca is deep in the legendary coal mining area of South Wales, the chief industry when the town began to emerge as such was brick making. Unlike many of the surrounding towns there was little ironstone close to Risca, but there was clay in abundance, clay for both house and fire bricks. During the second quarter of the 19th century Risca therefore became the centre for the South Wales brick industry. Over the course of the next hundred years numerous brickworks arose along the River Ebbw and the Monmouthshire and Brecon Canal. The Darren brickworks, the first to be constructed, produced over one million bricks in its first four years. With the exception of one works (owned by the seemingly inappropriately named Fergus Brain) all the brickworks were a resounding success.

To heat their kilns the brickwork owners used local coal. In the last two decades of the 18th century coal had been mined in the area by a company owned by children of Charles Phillips, the local squire. Phillips was one of the larger-than-life people that the British are renowned for producing, a giant of a man standing 6 feet 4 inches

(1.93 metres). He was famous as a hunting man and once presented 12 pairs of his own hounds to George III at Windsor. A local story tells that while out hunting one day he wagered that he could jump a canal lock on horseback. Apparently he almost made it, landing head first on the far side. For his failure he not only lost his bet, but spent the rest of his life with a metal plate in his head. It appears that eight children were involved in the coal mining venture, a great number you might think, but only a small fraction of the total, as Phillips could call on 26 in all.

Within the town there are several buildings of enormous interest. The Male Voice Choir and Collieries Institute buildings are marvellous examples of the proud style of local folk, while the Moriah Baptist and Trinity Methodist are superb Non-conformist chapels.

Walk Directions   [-] denotes Point of Interest

1. Follow Darren Road, with the houses on your right. At its end, bear right, uphill, along a track which becomes rougher as it rises, but rises through beautiful woodland. The huge trees here, and the unspoilt country in the tight stream valley to the left, give a glimpse of how much of South Wales looked before the beginning of the coal and steel industries. When a track is reached on the right (just after the buildings of Sheep Wash, down and left) look to the left to see a stile signed for the Raven Walk: this will be taken on the return. Continue up the track, but where it bears left to Hansons Lodge and levels out, take the signed path ahead, following it on to the flank of Twmbarlwm from where a steep path leads up right to the fort at the summit [1].

2. Reverse the route to Sheep Wash and turn right over the stile. Follow the grassy path beyond down to the stream. Cross a stile and follow the path uphill into the wood. At the fence corner, turn left and walk with the wood on your left and open country on your right to reach the ruins of Cwmbyr Farm.

3. Cross a stile and bear left, downhill, soon reaching a path junction. Turn left and follow the path downhill through the wood to reach a

'packhorse' bridge over the Monmouthshire and Brecon Canal [2]. Cross the bridge and turn left along the path beside it, the old towpath, to return to Darren Road.

4. If the alternative start has been used, or to extend your walk into Risca [3], follow the road, then bear right to return to the canal (which has been blocked at Darren Road), following the path beside it to reach Temperance Hill and Navigation Road [2]. Follow the road downhill, going around one hairpin bend and under the railway to reach St Mary's Church. Continue to the main road and turn left to reach Risca. It is also possible to continue along the canal, turning right later to drop down into the town.

Facilities

There is a full range of facilities in Risca.

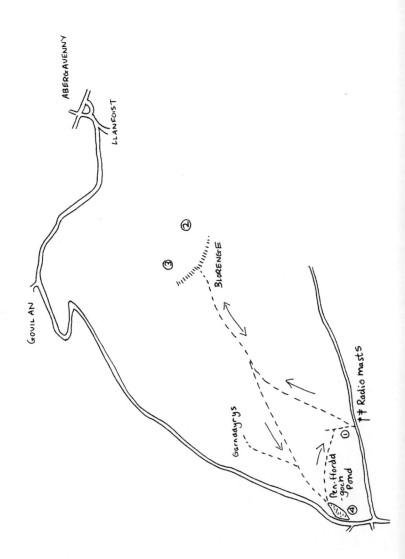

ABERGAVENNY

LLANFOIST

GOVILAN

② ③

BLORENGE

Garnddyrys

Pen-ffordd
-goch
Pond

① ④

┬╪ Radio masts

Blorenge

OS Maps:	Landranger Sheet 161 (Abergavenny and the Black Mountains) Outdoor Leisure Sheet 13 (Brecon Beacons National Park- Eastern Area)
Start:	At Grid Reference 264107 , opposite the radio masts at the southern edge of Blorenge Mountain
Access:	The masts lie beside an unfenced road which heads down into the Usk Valley from the B4246 Blaenafon to Govilon/Abergavenny road
Parking:	There is a car park at the start. Alternative parking is available close to Pen-ffordd-goch Pond
Grade:	Moderate - rough moorland with a limited number of paths. However, the route finding is very easy.

Points of Interest:

1. The starting car park is officially known as the Foxhunter Park because buried beneath the rocks to the north is the famous show-jumping horse Foxhunter. The horse was owned by Colonel Harry Llewellyn of Govilon, at the foot of Blorenge, and his famous victories are listed on a memorial plaque. The most famous was at the Helsinki Olympics of 1952 when Col Llewellyn and Foxhunter led the British team to the gold medal.

2. Below Blorenge's northern edge lies the Usk Valley. On the valley's southern side, Blorenge is the easternmost peak of the mountain range that dominates southern Wales (and which now forms the Brecon Beacons National Park). To the north Sugar Loaf and Ysgyryd Fawr are the easternmost peaks of the range that lie on the Usk Valley's northern side. To the west the valley is narrow, hemmed

in by the high peaks of Beacons Park, while to the east is a broad, flat coastal plain through which the river runs to reach the sea at Newport. The Romans were the first to recognise the extreme strategic importance of holding the entrance to the tight section of the Usk Valley: the valley was their route from Caerleon to Brecon. Soon after establishing their fort at Caerleon they built another where the Gavenny stream reached the Usk, calling it *Gobannium* after the stream. When the Normans came they too recognised the importance of the site and, in about 1090, they built the first castle at what is now Abergavenny. Following its construction the castle was the scene of several murderous encounters in a story of vengeance between rival Welsh and Norman families. One of the Norman lords of Abergavenny Castle was William de Braose, a grandson of Milo FitzWalter, an earlier lord. Gerald of Wales tells the story of de Braose's vengeance. He notes that de Braose invited Seisyll ap Dyfnwal, who had murdered one of Milo FitzWalter's sons, his son and some of his followers into the castle 'under a colourable pretext of communication'. Having gathered them together de Braose ordered them to take an oath 'that no traveller by the waie amongst them should beare any bow, or any other unlawful weapon'. Not surprisingly they refused and de Braose condemned them to death, a sentence that was immediately executed by his men. At the same time Seisyll's lands were attacked and another son was murdered. De Braose was clearly an unpleasant man as a later episode amply testifies. Following a quarrel with King John, de Braose fled to France. His wife and son were held in Corfe Castle probably against his return to face the King, but he did not return, his family dying of starvation.

3. On the southern side of the Usk, tucked in beneath Blorenge's lower slopes lie two 'trade routes' which were important in the industrial development of the area, one using the Usk Valley to penetrate the high peaks of what is now the Brecon Beacons National Park. The Brecon and Abergavenny Canal was begun in 1797, workers taking 15 years to complete its 33 mile (52 kilometres) length from Brecon to the Monmouthshire Canal at Pontymoel near Pontypool. It was surveyed and engineered by Thomas Dadford who was such a good

canal builder that he required only six locks along the entire length, five of these being in a short section near Llangynidr. The canal was a short-lived success: by the mid-19th century work had begun on the railways, and railways meant doom for canals. The canal fell into disrepair and would have been lost forever if a local canal society had not been formed to refurbish it. Now called the Brecon and Monmouthshire, the canal is popular with pleasure craft and is a haven for wildlife.

Govilon, the village at the base of Blorenge's northern slope, derives its name from *gefail*, forge, implying the existence of iron smelting from very early times. The nearby Clydach gorge had deposits of iron ore and plenty of wood for the charcoal needed for smelting. What was needed was a means of transportation from the Gorge to the canal. To do this a tramway was constructed, the trams being horse-drawn. With the development of coal for smelting, an ironworks was built at Nantyglo (at the top of the Gorge), and the tramway was extended to it, a remarkable feat of engineering as the route had an average gradient of only 1 in 38 despite the steepness of the Gorge. Later, the tramway was extended north of Abergavenny, carrying coal to Hereford and beyond, and when the railways came the tramway embankment was used to carry the line. During the early years of this century the line carried both freight and passengers, but it did not survive Dr Beeching's axe in 1958.

4. Although the Pen-ffordd-goch Pond looks natural it is in fact artificial having been constructed in the 18th century to supply water to an iron forge at Garnddyris, a little way to the north and down the hill. Garnddyris was one of the area's earliest forges using the local iron ore deposits and charcoal from the Clydach Gorge woods to smelt iron.

Walk Directions   [-] denotes Point of Interest

1. From the car park, take the stony track from its far end, soon reaching an outcrop of rocks where there is a horizontal memorial [1]. Step right to reach a memorial seat (to F J Hando) and follow the faint grassy path to reach the obvious scarred path through the heather.

Follow this path to the summit of Blorenge, at 1,834 feet (559 metres).

2. Although the summit is an excellent viewpoint of the Black Mountains, to the north, the Usk Plain, to the east, and the land to the south and west, it is not possible to look down into the Usk Valley because of the broad summit plateau stretching north-eastwards. Walk north-east, crossing rough, undulating moor to reach the edge of this plateau, then descending (still heading north-eastwards) to reach the edge of ground which falls steeply away towards Abergavenny [2] and Govilon [3].

3. After admiring the view, retrace your steps to the summit, then head south-westwards, avoiding the outward route, to reach Pen-ffordd-goch Pond [4].

4. Now head south-eastwards, avoiding the inlet streams to the pond, to return to the start.

Facilities

None of the route, but there is a full range in Blaenafon to the south.

Blaenafon

OS Maps: Landranger Sheet 161 (Abergavenny and the Black Mountains)
Outdoor Leisure Sheet 13 (Brecon Beacons National Park- Eastern Area)

Start: The Ironworks car park, Blaenafon.

Access: Blaenafon lies at the end of the A4043 road which follows Cwm Afon, the valley of the Afon Llwyd, from Pontypool.

Parking: The Ironworks car park, Blaenafon.

Grade: Easy - streets and good tracks.

Points of Interest:

1. It is doubtful whether a single town characterises the South Wales area better than Blaenafon, both in the geographic sense and in terms of industrial archaeology. The valley town of legend clings in terraced ranks to a steep hillside, the winding gear of the pit dominating some part of the scene. Blaenafon has its winding gear, though it is some way from the town, and its terraced ranks, though the valley side is not steep. Additionally it has the bleak uplands that characterised the area before the industrialisation of the valleys, and an enviable place in the history of that industrialisation.

The town lies close to ironstone deposits below the nearby moorland: there were forests on the sides of valley and the local streams were powerful enough to drive waterwheels which in turn drove bellows to produce the blast in iron smelters. There were forges here from the late 16th century, but eventually the forests were denuded. The outlook was very bleak, but the discovery, in the first half of the 18th century, of the use of coke as an alternative fuel for the smelting of iron came to the rescue. Now Blaenafon came into its own

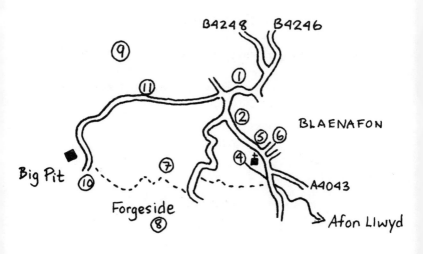

B4248   B4246

⑨

⑪

①

②

BLAENAFON

⑤ ⑥

④

Big Pit

⑩

⑦

A4043

Forgeside

⑧

Afon Llwyd

①

BLAENAFON
STREET ROUTE

②

⑤

③

⑥

④

for on the one site there was coal suitable for coking, iron ore, building stone and water. Additionally there was limestone which was used as a flux in the furnaces. In 1789 the first ironworks was built by Thomas Hill of Stafford with Benjamin Pratt of Worcestershire and the Welshman Thomas Hopkins. Five furnaces were built into the hillside so that they could be charged directly from above. Pig iron was moved on a balance tower where water was piped into a box until it was heavy enough to lift a trolley loaded with iron from the casting floor level up to 'moor' level and transportation. At the base the water was emptied and the water box was lifted back to the tower top by the weight of the descending pig trolley. Near the ironworks is a small square that once housed some of the workers. One side of the square is open on to the site itself. The two parallel sides contain the two-up, two-down cottages of craftsmen and their families, while the back row was the works offices on the ground floor and a dormitory for labourers above.

2. Ty Mawr was built for Samuel Hopkins, son of Thomas. The difference between the living conditions of the workers and the boss could hardly be greater and led to considerable anger. After Hopkins' death the house was used by directors of the company, not only as a 'hotel' when they were visiting the town, but as a shooting lodge in the grouse season, the directors shooting on Blorenge Mountain (see Walk 14), then the most southerly grouse moor in Britain.

3. St. Peter's School was built as a memorial to Samuel Hopkins by his sister Sarah in 1815, the first school in Wales to be specifically built by a company owner for the children of the workers. It is now disused, its Latin inscription crumbling away. It once noted that the school carried into effect 'the benevolent intentions of her deeply lamented and most deserving brother towards his Glenavonians'. The last word is clearly a spelling mistake, probably by a cutter who did not know Blaenafon well.

4. St Peter's Church was built by Hill and Hopkins in 1805. It is a simple local stone structure with a considerable quantity of cast iron work that makes it most interesting. Window frames and sills and tomb covers are of iron, as is the font, a feature which is unique.

5. The Workmen's Hall and Institute, the finest of its type in South Wales, is a monument to Blaenafon's early workers. It was built in 1894 in magnificent style, paid for by contributions from steelworkers and miners. The building had an auditorium for concerts and family shows, a games room, a library and a reading room.

6. The Horeb Chapel was built in 1862, the nearby Moriah Chapel in 1888. Non-conformism was prevalent in South Wales as the Anglican church ministers invariably sided with the mill and mine owners during disputes whereas the Non-conformist minsters maintained faith with the workers.

7. In the wake of the discovery of how to make quality steel from ore high in phosphorus (see [11] below) a new company was formed at Blaenafon but the difficulty in obtaining ore meant that steel production finally stopped in the town in 1938. The site is now owned by Doncasters. The memorial to Gilchrist Thomas was erected in 1960.

8. Forgeside was built in the mid-19th century to accommodate workers in the new ironworks and in the colliery. There was a 'green' at the centre, and shops, a school and pub were built to make the village independent of Blaenafon. In its original form, the streets were named A Row, B Row etc. Rows A and B were demolished in 1977.

9. In the earliest days of iron making at Blaenafon, iron ore (and, later, coal) was obtained by 'hushing' or scouring. Turf and top soil was loosened, then a dam was formed above the loosened area. A reservoir would be filled by local streams then, when it was full, the dam would be broken and the water would rush down the hillside, removing the loosened soil and revealing the ore. The process was inefficient and left scarring which can still be seen.

10. The Big Pit colliery was sunk in 1880 and produced coal until 1980. It then re-opened as a museum to coal mining. Visitors - who will need good footwear and warm clothing - are given a helmet with a lamp and descend a 90 metre/280 foot shaft to explore the underground world of pony stables, engine houses and coal seams. On the surface the old colliery buildings - winding engine-house, pit-head baths,

blacksmith's shop etc - can be explored. There is also a craft, book and souvenir shop and a licensed restaurant in the old miners' canteen.

It is all a far cry from coal mining's early days. In 1840 when a Parliamentary Commission was set up to investigate conditions in mines, they visited Blaenafon. What they found led directly to the Mines Act of 1842. In the pits they found women stripped to the waist hauling coal trams and young children performing critical functions underground for many hours alone each day. The Commission found a boy of seven, already a veteran of three years in the mine, who smoked a pipe all day in order to stay awake. The Commission reported to Parliament noting that in 1838, the latest year for which complete records were available, there had been (throughout Britain) 58 deaths of children under 13 and 62 more of children from 13 to 18. But Parliament was not impressed, some members claiming that to ban children from the mines would bring about the collapse of the industry. Nevertheless the Mines Act was passed forbidding women, and girls and boys under ten, to work underground. Ironically it was opposed by not only the mine owners, but the families, who needed the money, and ignored. When inspectors were appointed in 1850 the first inspector at Blaenafon turned out 70 women and children and was promptly besieged by the women angry at their loss of income.

11. In 1856 the work of Bessemer and Siemens had allowed steel to replace iron as the primary constructional metal. However the processes could only produce good quality steel, that is metal not susceptible to brittle fracture, from low phosphorus ores which constituted only 10 per cent of all known deposits. The problem of how to remove phosphorus from normal ores was unsolved, and apparently insoluble, for 20 years until experiments at Blaenafon showed the way. The experiments were carried out by Sidney Gilchrist Thomas, not a chemist or even someone employed at Blaenafon. He was, in fact, a clerk at the Metropolitan Police Courts. Thomas was a keen amateur chemist and was obsessed by the problem of phosphoric steels. In 1876 his cousin, Percy Gilchrist, was appointed Chemist at Blaenafon, and Thomas began to carry out experiments on the plant at weekends. By 1878 Thomas and Gilchrist

had achieved the breakthrough. It revolutionised steel making immediately. Andrew Carnegie, the famous Scottish-American industrialist, declared 'These two young men, Thomas and Gilchrist of Blaenafon, did more for Britain's greatness than all the Kings and Queens put together. Moses struck the rock and brought forth water. They struck the useless phosphoric ore and transformed it into steel - a far greater miracle'. Sadly the hectic pre-discovery life involving endless travelling, poor diet and little sleep took its toll on Thomas and he became very ill. In 1885, aged just 35, he died in Paris. Today the town's industrial estate remembers the men in its name.

Walk Directions   [-] denotes Point of Interest

1. From the car park, with its massive steel press, return to the road. Opposite is the Blaenafon Ironworks [1]. Turn right and walk to a T-junction of roads. Turn right, following the road as it bends left. To the left is Ty Mawr [2]. Further on, on the right, is St Peter's School [3], and beyond it, St Peter's Church [4], with the Workmen's Hall and Institute opposite [5]. A short distance further on is the Horeb Chapel [6].

2. Continue along the road, passing another car park, also with a steel press, then bear right to cross a footbridge over the Afon Llwyd. Cross the road beyond and follow the metalled path up a series of steps to reach another road. Turn right, then first left past some old garages. At the top of the road, turn right. At the T-junction, turn left climbing to reach a sharp right bend. To the right is the site of the 'New Ironworks' [7].

3. Turn right with the road, passing the Forgeside Inn, on the left. Go past the Zion Baptist Chapel, then go left with the road. Now turn sharp right (Griffiths Court) to reach Row C in Forgeside [8]. At the end, turn left and continue up the road and then the steep concrete track ahead. Continue along this track as it bears right, with a fine view of the town and the scarred hillside beyond [9].

4. At the end of the track is Big Pit [10]. Go right along the access road - passing the entrance to the site on the left - following it to a T-

junction. Turn left under the railway bridge, following it past the Gilchrist Thomas Industrial Estate [11] to return to the start.

Facilities

There is a full range of facilities in Blaenafon.

Circular Walks
on Anglesey

WALKS WITH HISTORY

Circular Walks
in Central Wales

WALKS WITH HISTORY

Circular Walks
in the
Brecon Beacons
National Park

TOM HUTTON

Walks with History

If you want to experience the very best of Wales, then these are the books for you. The walks are graded and there is something for everybody – short walks for families and more demanding routes to satisfy even the most experienced hillwalker.

Walks on the Llŷn Peninsula
PART 1 - SOUTH & WEST – N. Burras & J. Stiff.
ISBN 0-86381-343-7; **£4.50**
This series combines walks with history, stories and legends. Pastoral walks as well as coastal & mountain panoramas.

Walks on the Llŷn Peninsula
PART 2 - NORTH & EAST – N. Burras & J. Stiff.
ISBN 0-86381-365-8: **£4.50**

Walks in the Snowdonia Mountains
– Don Hinson. 45 walks, mostly circular, 96 pages, inc. accurate maps and drawings. 96pp ISBN 0-86381-385-2; New Edition: **£3.75**

Walks in North Snowdonia
– Don Hinson. 100km of paths to help those wishing to explore the area further. 96pp ISBN 0-86381-386-0; New Edition; **£3.75**

New Walks in Snowdonia
– Don Hinson. 43 circular walks together with many variations. This book introduces you to lesser known paths and places which guide book writers seem to have neglected. Maps with every walk. Pen & ink drawings. 96pp ISBN 0-86381-390-9; New Edition; **£3.75**

Circular Walks in North Pembrokeshire
– Paul Williams, 14 walks, 112 pages. ISBN 0-86381-420-4; **£4.50**

Circular Walks in South Pembrokeshire
– Paul Williams, 14 walks, 120 pages. ISBN 0-86381-421-2; **£4.50**

From Mountain Tops to Valley Floors
Salter & Worral. ISBN 0-86381-430-1; **£4.50**
Detailed information for casual/family walks and for the more adventurous walker.

NEW FOR 1998:
Circular Walks in the Brecon Beacons National Park;
ISBN 0-86381-476-X; **£4.50**
Circular Walks on Anglesey; ISBN 0-86381-478-6; **£4.50**
Circular Walks in Gower; ISBN 0-86381-479-4; **£4.50**
Circular Walks in Central Wales; ISBN 0-86381-480-8; **£4.50**
Circular Walks in Gwent; ISBN 0-86381-477-8; **£4.50**

NEW WALKS IN GWYNEDD

From Mountain Tops to Valley Floors

DAVE SALTER & DAVE WORRALL

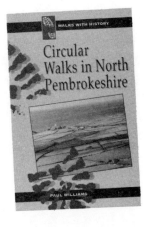

WALKS WITH HISTORY

Circular Walks in North Pembrokeshire

PAUL WILLIAMS

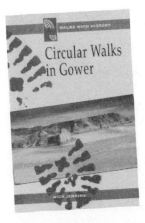

WALKS WITH HISTORY

Circular Walks in Gower

NICK JENKINS

Mountaineering & Botany

The Complete Guide to Snowdon/Yr Wyddfa
– Robert Joes. PVC Cover; ISBN 0-86381-222-8; **£6.95**

The Lakes of Eryri
– Geraint Roberts. Wildlife, fishing and folklore enhances this book aimed at anyone who loves Snowdonia. PVC cover; 256 pp; ISBN 0-86381-338-0; **£8.90**

The Mountain Walker's Guide to Wales
– Colin Adams. A comprehensive guide to 100 routes covering 200 Welsh peaks. 192 pp; ISBN 0-86381-154-X; Map, PVC Cover; **£6.90**

The Botanists and Guides of Snowdonia
– Dewi Jones. An account of the local guides and the plant hunters. 172 pp; ISBN 0-86381-383-6; **£6.95**

Travellers in Wales

Visitor's Delight
– Dewi Roberts. An anthology of visitor's impressions of North Wales. 152 pp; ISBN 0-86381-224-4; **£3.75**

The A-Z of Betws-y-coed
– Donald Shaw. Full of facts, stories and history about the popular Welsh resort. 136 pp; 0-86381-153-1; **£2.99**

Snowdonia, A Historical Anthology
– David Kirk. 60 writers portray the people and landscape of one of the most beautiful regions in Europe. 248 pp; ISBN 0-86381-270-8; **£5.95**

All the Days were Glorious
– Gwyn Neale. George Gissing in North Wales – quotes from Gissing's letters and diary. 56 pp; ISBN 0-86381-286-4; **£2.95**

The Land of Old Renown – George Borrow in Wales
– Dewi Roberts. A retrace of George Borrow's journey through Wales. ISBN 0-86381-436-0; **£4.50**

Both Sides of the Border
An Anthology of writing on the Welsh Border Region by Dewi Roberts. ISBN 0-86381-461-1; **£4.75**

A Tour in Wales by Thomas Pennant
An old classic abridged by David Kirk. 176 pp; ISBN 0-86381-473-5; **£5.75**

Revd John Parker's Tour of Wales and its Churches (1798-1860)
Abridged by Edgar W. Parry. ISBN 0 86381-481-6; **£4.75**

Aviation in Wales

Early Aviation in North Wales
– Roy Sloan. From early nineteenth century balloon flights to the outbreak of World War II. 168 pp; ISBN 0-86381-119-1; **£2.75**

Wings of War over Gwynedd
– Roy Sloan. Aviation in Gwynedd during World War II.
200 pp; ISBN 0-86381-189-2; **£4.50**

Aircraft Crashes in Gwynedd
– Roy Sloan. Flying accidents in Gwynedd 1910-1990.
168 pp; ISBN 0-86381-281-3; **£5.50**

Down in Wales
– Terence R. Hill. Visits to some war-time air crash sites.
94 quarto pp; ISBN 0-86381-283-X; **£6.50**

Down in Wales 2
– Terence R. Hill. More visits to air crash sites. ISBN 0-86381-401-8; **£6.95**

Welsh History

Donald Gregory's Series – Guides to historical locations with a brief history:

Wales Before 1066 – A Guide
144 pp; ISBN 0-86381-396-8; maps/illustrations; **£4.00**

Wales Before 1536 – A Guide
160 pp; ISBN 0-86381-250-3; maps/illustrations; **£4.50**

Wales After 1536 – A Guide
156 pp; ISBN 0-86381-318-6; maps/illustrations; **£4.95**

The Battles of Wales
– Dilys Gater. An account of battles on Welsh soil.
128 pp; ISBN 0-86381-178-7; **£3.00**

Historic Shipwrecks of Wales
– Dilys Gater. 136 pp; ISBN 0-86381-216-3; **£3.50**

The Young Republicans
– 'Gweriniaethwr'. A record of the Welsh Republican Movement.
184 pp; ISBN 0-86381-362-3; **£7.50**

The Day Before Yesterday
– Donald Gregory. Historical essays on the living past.
ISBN 0-86381-371-4; **£4.50**